PIVOTAL
MOMENTS
IN HISTORY

# MARCO POLO'S
# JOURNEY TO CHINA

## DIANA CHILDRESS

TWENTY-FIRST CENTURY BOOKS
MINNEAPOLIS

For Steve, from Venice to China and beyond,
traveling companion sans pareil

Acknowledgments: The author thanks Morris Rossabi, professor of Asian History at Columbia University and author of many books on Mongolia and Kublai Khan.

Primary source material in this text is printed over an antique-paper texture.

*The image on the cover is of the Polos leaving Venice to begin their journey to China. It is a print of a drawing from a fourteenth-century manuscript in the Bodleian Library at Oxford, England.*

Twenty-First Century Books
A division of Lerner Publishing Group, Inc.
241 First Avenue North
Minneapolis, MN 55407 U.S.A.

Website address: www.lernerbooks.com


Library of Congress Cataloging-in-Publication Data

Childress, Diana.
        Marco Polo's travels in China / by Diana Childress.
            p.    cm. — (Pivotal moments in history)
        Includes bibliographical references and index.
        ISBN-13: 978–0–8225–5903–0 (lib. bdg. : alk. paper)
        ISBN-10: 0–8225–5903–X (lib. bdg. : alk. paper)
            1. Polo, Marco, 1254–1323?—Juvenile literature. 2. Voyages and travels—Juvenile
    literature. 3. China—Description and travel—Juvenile literature. I. Title.
    G370.P9C48  2008
    910.4—dc22                                                                           2005024003

Manufactured in the United States of America
1 2 3 4 5 6 – DP – 13 12 11 10 09 08

# CONTENTS

# CHAPTER ONE
# VENICE, ISLAND CITY OF MERCHANTS

Venice today is the most beautiful and pleasant city in the world. . . . You will find abundant food here, bread and wine, chickens and ducks, fresh and salted meat, fish from the sea and from rivers, and merchants from every country selling and buying. In this fair city you will see gentlemen, old and young, renowned for their nobility, merchants, bankers, artisans, seamen of all kinds, and ships to sail in every direction and war galleys to harm her enemies. You will meet fair ladies, too, women and girls, in abundance, all dressed most richly.

—Martino da Canale, Les Estoires de Venise (The History of Venice), 1275

The urge to explore, to travel and to learn about other countries and people and even to fly out into space to see what lies beyond Earth is so common today that it is hard to imagine a time when few people ventured more than a day's walk from their homes. The story of how the inward-looking, farming culture of the European Middle Ages (A.D. 476 to 1453) became the restless, inquisitive, and expansionist society that pushed its way into every continent goes back to the thirteenth century. Many factors contributed to the rise of Europe and, later, the United States as world powers. But one key moment in that seismic shift was the day in 1271 when Marco Polo, a bright, curious teenager, sailed out of Venice on a twenty-four-year journey to China. The middle-aged man who returned to Venice was bursting with newfound knowledge to share. The book he wrote about Asia (known in English as *The Travels of Marco Polo*) was a pivotal moment that changed the world.

*A fifteenth-century book that describes the government of Venice includes this view of the city.*

When Marco Polo was born in 1254, Venice was a glittering city, a magical kingdom rising at high tide out of a shimmering expanse of water. With a population of around one hundred thousand people, it was one of the biggest, busiest, and wealthiest cities in western Europe.

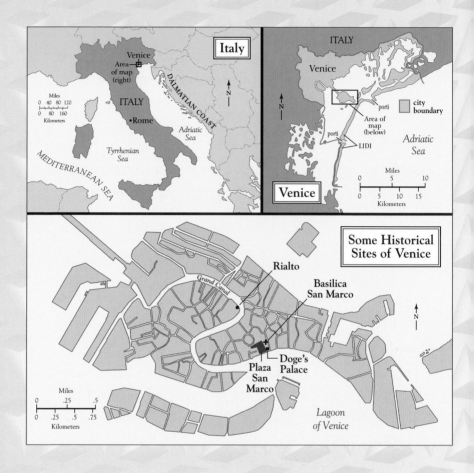

Venice stands on 118 small, flat islands packed closely together in a shallow, crescent-shaped lagoon tucked into the northeastern coast of Italy. A barrier of narrow sandbanks protects the lagoon from stormy seas and enemy ships.

Through gaps between the sandbars, the tide carries salt water from the Adriatic Sea in and out of the lagoon. The ebbing and flowing water cuts deep channels, giving ships access to the city. At high tide, the lagoon is all water. At low tide, much of it turns into mud flats spread with seaweed and crisscrossed with waterways. A boat floating in one of these channels looks from a distance as if it is moving through fields.

## THE HOME OF SEABIRDS

In the days of the Roman Empire (27 B.C. to A.D. 476), the islands and the marshy mainland adjoining the lagoon were quiet backwaters. People living there fished, hunted for waterfowl, and made salt from the seawater. A Roman official wrote that their homes were like those of seabirds "stretching far away among the waters." They hitched their ships to the walls, he noted, just as mainlanders do their horses.

In the sixth century, Venice and other ports on the northeastern coast of Italy became part of the Byzantine Empire (A.D. 527 to 1453), which included what are now Greece, Albania, Macedonia, Bulgaria, and Turkey. The capital of the Byzantine Empire, Constantinople (modern Istanbul, Turkey), lay on both sides of the passageway between the Mediterranean and the Black seas, half in Europe, half in Asia. Its navy dominated both seas. Venetians elected their own leader, called a doge, but his official role was to represent the Byzantine Empire.

## VENICE AND BYZANTIUM: PROFITABLE TIES

For centuries Constantinople was the center of trade for both luxury goods from Asia and raw materials from Europe. With no land to farm, Venice depended entirely on trading salt and fish for other goods. Its political ties to

This illustration from a fourteenth-century French manuscript shows Constantinople some years after Marco Polo's return from China.

Constantinople gave the island traders a chance to grow rich. From Constantinople, Venetians purchased silks, cloth of gold, spices, perfumes, and medicines and took them to Italian trade fairs. A Swiss monk, writing in the late ninth century, described Venetian traders in the Italian city of Pavia as selling peacock feathers, fine fabrics from Tyre (in what is now Lebanon), embroidered silks, and ermine skins.

## QUEEN OF THE ADRIATIC

In 1000 Venetians cleared the Adriatic Sea of pirates by conquering cities along the coast of Dalmatia (a region that includes today's Slovenia and Croatia), where pirates had their bases. The victory brought Venice new sources of grain and more trading ports.

With the pirates subdued, Venetian trade increased. Merchants from Venice settled in ports around the eastern Mediterranean to oversee their international businesses. Everywhere they went, Venetians figured out what products local people wanted and then they provided them. In boats propelled by both oars and sails, Venetians carried timber, iron tools, and weapons from Germany; olive oil from Greece; pepper and cinnamon from southeastern Asia; cotton cloth from Egypt; porcelain and silk from China; carpets from Persia; and slaves and furs from Russia. One Venetian trading ship called itself *The Whole World*, probably because at one time or another it contained goods from every area known at that time.

Venetian wealth grew, and the city grew with it. In the mid-eleventh century, the doge's private chapel was torn down to make way for a much grander church with five domes. The new church, the Basilica San Marco—Saint Mark's Cathedral—contained the remains of the Christian apostle Saint Mark. The church was still being added to when Marco Polo was growing up. It remains a world-famous Venetian landmark.

## PROFITING FROM THE CRUSADES

During the Crusades (1096–1291), kings and noblemen from northern Europe hired Venetian galleys to transport knights, horses, and bowmen across the Mediterranean to what Christians called the Holy Land (which included coastal areas

# THE CRUSADES

In 1095 European leaders, urged on by the pope, began the Crusades, a series of wars to gain control of the city of Jerusalem and other Christian holy sites at the eastern end of the Mediterranean Sea. At the time, this area was under Muslim rule. After establishing Christian kingdoms in the Holy Land, however, the Europeans began to lose some of them to a well-organized Muslim offensive. Two more Crusades in the twelfth century regained little of the lost territory. In 1200 the pope called for a fourth Crusade, but the French and the Venetians attacked Constantinople instead. Five more Crusades took place during the thirteenth century, but none succeeded in establishing a lasting Christian kingdom. In 1291 Acre, the last Crusader stronghold, fell.

of southern Turkey, Syria, Lebanon, and Israel). In exchange, Venice earned the right to trade in the principal ports of the kingdoms that the Crusaders established. Tyre and Haifa and Acre (in Israel) became major centers of Venetian trade.

Other port cities also supplied ships for the Crusaders, especially Genoa and Pisa. A strong rivalry developed among the three Italian cities as they started trading colonies in the Crusader states.

In the early thirteenth century, French leaders sent envoys to Venice to charter ships and food supplies for forty-five hundred knights and twenty thousand foot soldiers for a

Fourth Crusade. Enrico Dandolo, the doge at the time, was old and blind, but he saw a golden opportunity for Venice. He named a very low price and even offered to protect the convoy with fifty Venetian war galleys—free of charge. He had only one condition: that Venice "shall take the half of all that is conquered, whether in territory or in money, by land or by sea."

The ten thousand French Crusaders who reached Venice couldn't pay for their passage. The wily Dandolo proposed to forgive the debt if the French army would help him conquer

This illustration shows merchants in a seaport on the Mediterranean Sea. It is based on a painting in a manuscript of The Travels of Marco Polo, the book Polo wrote about his journey to China.

the port city of Zara (modern Zadar, Croatia) on the Dalmatian coast, which was then controlled by the king of Hungary. The French leaders agreed, and a well-armed fleet soon captured the city.

The French and the Venetians then became involved in a struggle to control the Byzantine Empire. In the summer of 1204, they succeeded in taking Constantinople and crowned a new emperor. But when the Venetians and the French Crusaders settled down for the winter there, planning to set sail for the Holy Land in the spring, war broke out anew. They managed to hold the city, and in a frenzy of revenge and greed, they looted its fabulous wealth.

## CONSTANTINOPLE SACKED

The plundering of Constantinople by the French and the Venetians in 1204 was one of the greatest losses of artistic treasures in history. Objects of gold, silver, and bronze were melted down; precious stones were torn from altarpieces and chalices. Art that was not destroyed was loaded onto Venetian galleys and brought back in triumph to decorate Venice. The most visible of the treasures looted by the Venetians were the four gold-coated bronze horses taken from atop the stadium where chariot races were held. These splendid steeds were hoisted up over the doors of the church of San Marco for everyone to see.

The balance of power in the eastern Mediterranean was tipping westward. Constantinople's star was sinking. Venice's was rising. The island city-state of merchants had become a world power.

The Italian artist Domenico Tintoretto (1560–1635) painted his version of the conquest of Constantinople by the French and Venetians almost four hundred years after the city's fall.

## GROWING UP IN VENICE'S GLORY DAYS

Over the next fifty years, the Venetian economy boomed. Almost every citizen benefited—or hoped to. In other parts of Europe, the nobility held large tracts of land and looked down their noses on merchants who grew rich on trade. In Venice the nobles, including the doge himself, engaged in commerce. Commoners and priests also invested in trading ventures. Men willing to do the traveling and negotiating did not need to put up any cash. If the journey was successful, they earned one-quarter of the profits. A pilgrim traveling through Venice remarked, "The entire people are merchants!"

# STOLEN HORSES

The great bronze horses *(below)* that the Venetians took from Constantinople also attracted another famous looter. In 1797, after seizing control of northern Italy, French emperor Napoleon shipped the horses to Paris. They were restored to Venice after Napoleon's defeat at the Battle of Waterloo in 1815.

These famous horses moved again in the 1970s. After noticing that industrial pollution from the mainland was damaging the bronze, the Venetians placed them in a museum inside the Basilica San Marco. The horses that now prance atop the entrance to the Basilica San Marco are copies.

Among the many nobles who formed private trading companies were the three Polo brothers: Marco, Nicolo, and Maffeo. Legal documents show that their business was spread across at least three cities. Besides their home in Venice, the family had property in Constantinople and in Soldaia, a Black Sea port known today as Sudak, Ukraine.

Nicolo had a son, also named Marco. This Marco Polo is the one who later wrote the famous work, known in English as *The Travels*. One manuscript (hand-written copy) of that book says that when Marco was born in 1254, his father and Uncle Maffeo were away on business and that they did not see him until he was fifteen.

We can only imagine what it was like for a young boy to grow up watching the ships and traders arrive in the busy port city of Venice, hoping for his father's return and dreaming of the time when he too would be sailing away to distant lands. He and his mother probably lived with the Polo family in the house near the rivulet of San Severo that the elder Marco mentioned in his will. After his mother died, sometime before 1269, young Marco would have been looked after by other relatives, perhaps his grandmother or his Aunt Flora and her husband.

Thirteenth-century Venice was an exciting place to grow up. Just a few hundred yards south of Marco's home were the docks where galleys unloaded cargoes from faraway lands. To the west lay the Rialto, the commercial center of Venice. Here crowds of foreign merchants, dressed in foreign fashions and speaking many languages, warehoused and traded their goods. Shops of artisans spilled out into narrow footpaths, where nobles on horseback and drivers of pack

## DALMATIAN ORIGINS

According to an early editor of Marco Polo's book, the Polo family came from the seaport city of Shibenik in what is now Croatia. He says that they moved from there to Venice in 1033, 221 years before Marco's birth. Whether these Polos were of Slavic or Latin descent is not known. Since Roman times, people had been trading and settling back and forth across the narrow Adriatic Sea.

mules picked their way. Money changers set up business in narrow stalls where they bought and sold gold, silver, or bronze coins from different cities. Merchants struck deals over pearls from India, jewels from Sri Lanka, and bales of silk, muslin, and brocade from Baghdad and Mosul (Iraq), and China. Notaries recorded details of contracts being drawn up for future voyages.

Prosperity was beautifying the city. Elegant stone mansions called palazzi were beginning to line the main waterway, the Grand Canal, which snakes in a backward S through the heart of the city. In 1264 the public square in front of the Doge's Palace leading to the docks was paved for the first time. At the Rialto, workers were driving wooden piles deep into the mud of the Grand Canal to support a new, larger wooden bridge that curved upward to allow ships to pass beneath.

In the arch over the central doorway of San Marco, stoneworkers carved a vivid calendar that shows people

working at different tasks for each month of the year. Inside the cathedral, craftsmen pieced together thousands of tiny glass fragments to create mosaic pictures that glittered with gold. The walls gleamed with scenes from the Bible and legends of the saints. Up high in the enormous central dome of the church, one mosaic displayed Jesus rising into heaven.

*The Rialto Bridge spans the busy Grand Canal in this Italian painting from the late fifteenth century.*

## A MERCHANT'S EDUCATION

Young Marco did not attend school—Venice had none. Well-to-do parents hired teachers to tutor their children at home, often with their cousins or other neighborhood youngsters. They learned to read at the age of five or six. The Polos perhaps owned a few books, which were expensive. They were hand-written on pages made of scraped calfskin. Reading lessons focused on moral precepts and religion, but children also pored over stories about knights in armor, fabulous voyages, and legends about Alexander the Great (356–323 B.C.), whose conquests reached from Macedonia south to Egypt and across southwest Asia to Afghanistan. Marco later mentioned some of these legends in his book.

To become successful merchants, sons of Venetian nobles also learned arithmetic. In 1202 Leonardo Fibonacci, a mathematician from Pisa, introduced Arabic numerals (1,

# READING ROMAN NUMERALS

Although Europeans were beginning to use Arabic numerals in Polo's lifetime, the old habit of Roman numerals did not die out. In reading primary sources, it is helpful to know them. Here is a guide to how the Romans used seven letters to represent numbers:

I = 1; II = 2; III = 3; IIII or IV = 4; V = 5; X = 10; L = 50; C = 100; D = 500; M = 1000.

To write a number, say 520, start with the letter representing the largest digit, D. Anything after it (written on the right) is added to it. DXX = 500 + 10 + 10 = 520.

If a letter representing a smaller number appears first, it is subtracted from the larger one to its right. For example: IX = 10 − 1 = 9. Other examples: 7 = VII; 19 = XIX; 49 = XLIX; 470 = CCCCLXX or CDLXX; 550 = DL; 1254 = MCCLIV; 1996 = MCMXCVI; 2008 = MMVIII.

2, 3, and so on, as opposed to Roman numerals, I, II, III) to Europeans. Hand-written copies of his *Book of the Abacus* circulated throughout Europe.

A student notebook from fourteenth-century Venice gives an idea of the kinds of lessons Marco Polo learned. In about half of the notebook, the student wrote out math problems that merchants might face, such as determining how to distribute profits among three partners who have invested different amounts in a venture. After each question, he added an explanation of how to solve the problem.

The same notebook is crammed with lists of weights and measures used in different ports, ranging from Tunis in North Africa to Constantinople, and how these compare to the weights and measures used in Venice. A merchant had to know all these variations to avoid being cheated. The regulations concerning the size of bales of cloth in various European countries fill several pages. Students probably memorized all these sizes because in many ports, bales of cloth substituted for money.

The student also wrote down how to evaluate the various goods merchants bought and sold. Ginger, according to the notebook, should be long, smooth, and firm. A merchant should cut a sample open to check the color: "white," it says, "is better than dark."

This practical education included information about the calendar, astrology, various remedies for common ailments, charms to ward off evil before a voyage, and a smattering of history from the birth of Adam to A.D. 1303. Although we know nothing about who wrote this notebook or the sources of the information it contains, it provides clues to the kinds of things Marco Polo learned as he was growing up.

It is possible that Marco Polo himself kept such a notebook with all the important information he would need when he joined his father and uncles in their business. Much of the rest of Marco's education was probably hands on, learning about commerce by working with older relatives engaged in trade.

## A CELEBRATION OF VENICE

Childhood in medieval Venice meant taking part in its many festivals. Saints' days or days marking events in the life of Christ called for solemn masses, parades, and feasting. Saint Mark, the patron saint of the city, was honored four times a year—in April, in June, in October, and especially on January 31. This date marked the anniversary of the arrival of Saint Mark's body in Venice in 828 after two Venetians stole it from Alexandria, Egypt. According to Martino da Canale, five hundred small children carried banners and one hundred older children carried silver crosses in the January 31 celebrations.

In 1268, the year Marco was fourteen, the doge died. Forty-one electors chosen from among the Venetian nobility met in secret until twenty-five of them could agree on the man to be their next leader. They elected a naval hero, Lorenzo Tiepolo, who seven years earlier had led Venetians to two victories over Genoa, Venice's rival in trade.

When the bells of San Marco announced the decision, Venetians hurried to the piazza (square) to find out who it would be. From a balcony of the cathedral, an elector

This eighteenth-century Italian painting depicts the ceremonies marking a newly elected Venetian doge. The ceremonies are taking place in Saint Mark's Square with the cathedral in the background, as they would have in Marco Polo's time.

declared "Messer Lorenzo Tiepolo has been made doge!" The crowd surged into the cathedral to see officials dress Tiepolo in the ducal robes as he took the oath of office and received the golden banner of Saint Mark.

The celebrations lasted a week. Witness da Canale seems to be bursting with pride as he describes the wealth and glamour of the event in his book. No doubt other Venetians, among them fourteen-year-old Marco Polo, shared his view. Surely Venice was the grandest, richest, most beautiful city in the world!

## CHAPTER TWO
# THE FABULOUS EAST

For three days' journey from Changan [Xian, China]
the traveler passes through a fine country full of
thriving towns and villages, living by commerce and
industry. . . . Then he reaches the splendid city of
Kinsai [Hangzhou, China], whose name means "City
of Heaven." It well merits a description because it is
without doubt the finest and most splendid city in
the world.

—*Marco Polo*, The Travels, *1299*

The Venetians were proud of their city. Other Europeans
considered them arrogant, greedy, ruthless, and far too
focused on commerce. But the Venetians did not let
criticism from envious neighbors bother them. They were
confident of their superiority. Little did they imagine that
some 6,000 miles (10,000 kilometers) away, as the crow flies,
in what is now called China, were cities much larger and
grander than their own.

# "THE CITY OF HEAVEN"

Hangzhou (which Marco Polo called Kinsai) was only one of many great Chinese cities that flourished in the 1200s. This busy port at the head of a bay opening into the East China Sea was not 100 miles (160 km) in circumference nor did it boast twelve thousand bridges, as Polo's book says. These are either exaggerations or mistakes made by a scribe copying an early manuscript that no longer survives. But it was far larger than Venice. The walls around Hangzhou measured about 11 miles (18 km). Crowded into this space and spilling out over the walls, the population in the 1270s was one million—or ten times that of Venice. At the time, it was probably the world's largest city.

Polo marveled at its wide, spacious streets and waterways. "On one side is a lake of fresh water, very clear. On the other is a huge river, which entering by many channels, diffused throughout the city, carries away all its filth and then flows into the lake, from which it flows out toward the Ocean."

As in Venice, people got around in the city by land or water. But unlike Venice with its narrow wooden bridges, most of Hangzhou's 347 bridges were built of stone. Horses and carts easily crossed these bridges, yet they rose high enough for boats to pass beneath. The main avenue leading through the city from one end to the other was nine cart tracks wide, or about 50 feet (15 meters) across—twice the width of Roman roads in western Europe. Like all the streets of the city—and even some of the highways of China—it was paved with stone slabs and bricks. Along this street, Polo says, gentlemen and ladies rode in "a continuous procession of long carriages decked with awnings and cushions of silk."

The number of people amazed Polo. "Here at every hour of the day are crowds of people going to and fro on their own business, so that anyone seeing such a multitude would believe it a stark impossibility that food could be found to fill so many mouths." He was equally struck by the abundant, well-organized markets, where "forty to fifty thousand" traders sold "everything that could be desired to sustain life." To impress his readers with the quantity of food involved, he

A Chinese silk scroll painting from about the time Marco Polo visited China shows a scene of busy city life.

cited official records: "the pepper consumed daily in the city of Kinsai for its own use amounts to 43 cart-loads, each cart-load consisting of 223 lb. [100 kilograms]."

Polo's merchant's eye also noticed the "large stone buildings, in which all the merchants who come from India and elsewhere store their wares and merchandise." Chinese sources say that some of these storage facilities had more than one thousand rooms. To prevent any fire from spreading, water surrounded each building, and guards patrolled day and night to protect against burglars.

Hangzhou was home to many famous Buddhist monasteries and one Christian church. "Stately mansions with their gardens" lined the main street. The most impressive sight was Hangzhou's lake. Chinese poets and artists have celebrated this beautiful artificial lake since the seventh century. Pleasure boats with names such as *Hundred*

# OOPS!

One oddity of Polo's description of Kinsai is that Polo does not mention the city's twelve gates. On each stood a stone watchtower, where guards marked the passing hours with a gong and kept an eye out for fires and criminal activity. Instead, Polo's book places the guards on each of the "12,000 bridges." Historian A. C. Moule has suggested that an early copyist mistook "xii portes" (12 gates) for "xii ponts" (12 bridges). He must also have added an *m* to indicate one thousand. Twelve bridges probably did not sound sensational enough.

*Flowers, Ten Embroideries,* and *Jewels* carried crowds of merrymakers. People picnicked on wooded islands or dined in elegant pavilions overlooking the lake and enjoyed views of "temples, palaces, monasteries, and gardens with towering trees, running down to the water's edge."

## A FLOURISHING ECONOMY

Hangzhou was only the largest of many big cities in thirteenth-century China. During the Song dynasty (from 960 to 1234 in northern China and to 1279 in southern China), China's population increased rapidly. Official censuses show that it reached 100 million in the early twelfth century.

Much of this growing population farmed the rich agricultural land of the Chang River (or Yangtze River, as its lower reaches are called). Farmers traded their produce along rivers and canals. The Grand Canal of China, originally constructed in the sixth and seventh centuries and improved and extended in 1293, provided a major inland waterway more than 1,000 miles (1,600 km) long. It stretched between the northern city of Da-du (called Khanbalik by the Mongols and currently Beijing) and Hangzhou. Along the way, it linked the two largest rivers in Asia, the Chang and the Huang, as well as many smaller waterways. On the banks of this canal and especially at intersections of the canal and important rivers lay many of the "great and splendid" cities that Polo enumerated in his book.

Riverboats carried silk fabrics, porcelain dishes, wooden lacquerware, salt, tea, and a variety of foods from city to city. Outward from this thriving region, fleets of small ships plied

This Chinese painting from the period of Marco Polo's visit shows rice farmers at work.

the coast between ports on the East and the South China seas, while oceangoing junks rode the monsoon winds to trade in the East Indies, India, southwestern Asia, and eastern Africa.

The seaport at Zaiton (modern Quanzhou) astounded Polo even more than Hangzhou. At this port, about 400 miles (645 km) south of Hangzhou, many foreign ships came to trade. It was "the port for all the ships that arrive from India laden with costly wares and precious stones of great price and big pearls of fine quality," Polo wrote. "It is also a port for the merchants of Manzi [southern China] . . . so that the total amount of traffic in gems and other merchandise entering and leaving this port is a marvel to behold."

The port was such a major source of silk cloth in Europe that the English word *satin* is derived from its name. The number of ships was staggering. Polo assures his readers that "for one spice ship that goes to Alexandria [in Egypt] or elsewhere to pick up pepper for export to Christendom, Zaiton is visited by a hundred."

The ships themselves also captured Polo's attention. No small two-masted Venetian galleys sailed into Zaiton, only big four- and six-masted vessels, with sturdy double hulls and 150- to 300-man crews. Four seamen, not two, manned each oar. He admired how the ships' holds were divided into watertight compartments. That way, if part of a ship's hull struck a reef, cargo in other areas suffered no water damage.

## MYTHS OF THE EAST: MONSTERS, DRAGONS, AND UNICORNS

Europeans, however, knew nothing of the great cities and wealth of China before Polo's book. Before the thirteenth century, few Christians from Europe traveled farther east than the Holy Land or ports along the Black Sea. China was still thousands of miles away, the other side of a vast region dominated by Islamic rulers. Venice's Rialto was crowded with Germans, Armenians, Slavs, and other foreign merchants but no one from India or China. Instead, caravans from central Asia and the Arabian Peninsula brought Chinese porcelain and silks and Indian pepper and cinnamon to Black Sea and Mediterranean ports, where Venice and other Italian cities had trading stations. As a result, although

# CHINA'S MAJOR RIVERS

The Chang (also known as the Yangtze River), 3,964 miles (6,380 km) long, is the longest river in Asia.

The Huang (also known as the Yellow River), 3,395 miles (5,460 km) long, is the second-longest river in Asia.

Europeans enjoyed a variety of Asian products, they had little knowledge of the countries that produced these goods or of the people living in those distant lands.

With no up-to-date information in Europe about Asia, Europeans learned geography from legends based on the Bible, on other religious writings from the early Christian period, and on historical events such as the ancient conquests of Alexander the Great. Rumors, hearsay, and misinformation about Asia filled medieval encyclopedias.

Tales of monstrous creatures—rather like modern stories of extraterrestrials—helped to make up for the lack of facts. In the distant East, medieval writers claimed, lived cynocephali, people who had the heads of dogs. Sciopods hopped around on only one leg and used their single foot as a sunshade on hot days. Blemmyae had heads that grew beneath their shoulders.

Strange beasts also lurked in these faraway lands. Europeans already knew about elephants and camels. Their kings had received such animals as gifts from Asian rulers, and commoners came to stare. Having seen these odd animals, Europeans found it easy to believe that dragons,

Medieval writers in Europe told tales of Eastern monsters that included dog-headed people, humans with a single leg, and others with heads beneath their shoulders. These were all illustrated (above) in a manuscript version of Marco Polo's travels from 1400.

unicorns, and griffins, which had eagles' heads and wings attached to lions' bodies, also lived there. As a child in Venice, Marco Polo saw griffins pictured in stone carvings on the outer walls of San Marco Cathedral.

## NEWS OF CHRISTIAN ASIA— AND A SAPPHIRE BED

In the twelfth century, a man claiming to be a Christian leader from Asia met with the pope in Rome and told him of large Christian communities in the East. Many Christians did live in Asia. Most followed the teachings of Nestorius, a Greek who was a church leader in Constantinople in the fifth century. This man, Patriarch John of India, apparently wanted to reestablish ties with Western Christianity. Nothing came of the meeting, and modern scholars debate whether John was a real Nestorian clergyman or an impostor.

Another Asian priest named John captured more attention. A letter, allegedly from this priest, circulated widely in Europe, beginning in the late twelfth century. The author claimed to be Prester John, the ruler of a large, wealthy empire beyond the Tigris River, which flows out of Turkey and into Iraq. His subjects were devout Christians, he said, eager to recapture Jerusalem from the Muslims.

The letter was a hoax, but Europeans wanted desperately to believe in this valuable ally, for Muslim forces were attacking Crusader kingdoms in the Holy Land. What made the letter especially popular was the long description of Prester John's fabulous realm. It was truly a Utopia, a land of milk and honey, where "emeralds, sapphires, carbuncles, topazes, chrysolites, onyxes, beryls, sardonyxes, and many other precious stones" lay on a river bottom and no one ever told a lie or stole anything. Prester John lived in a crystal palace, slept in a sapphire bed, and ate off an emerald dining table. Marvelous stones and fountains cured all illnesses, and salamanders spun cocoons of amazing fireproof fibers.

During the early thirteenth century, new reports reached Europe about lands beyond the Muslim-controlled lands in Asia. A King David, allegedly the son or grandson of Prester

John, was making war on the Muslims. He had captured
Samarkand and other central Asian cities in modern
Uzbekistan, Turkmenistan, Afghanistan, and Iran.

## GENGHIS KHAN AND THE RISE OF THE MONGOLS

The reports were wrong. In fact, the powerful ruler who was
overthrowing Muslim rule in central Asia was not a
Christian. He was the Mongol leader Temujin, who in 1206
united the nomadic tribes of what is now Mongolia and took the title Genghis Khan (Very Mighty Lord). He then embarked on a series of conquests from central Asia to northern China. By the time of his death in 1227, Mongol rule stretched across Asia from northern China west to the Caspian Sea.

In the 1230s, Europeans finally realized that the Mongols were not the Christian allies they had hoped for. After Genghis Khan's death, his son Ogodei carried on his conquests. In 1237

In the 1200s, Genghis Khan united
the Mongol tribes of Mongolia and
conquered much of Asia.

Mongol armies invaded Russia, seizing Moscow and Kiev. They later marched into Poland and from there attacked Hungary in 1241.

Mongol armies were the foremost fighting forces in the world. Their key weapon was their cavalry. Mongol horsemen were skilled archers who could shoot arrows with deadly accuracy at a fast gallop. A favorite tactic was to charge into battle, arrows flying, then turn and seem to flee. When their retreat attracted pursuers, they pivoted in their saddles and shot them down.

The heavily armored knights and poorly trained foot soldiers of Europe were no match for the well-disciplined Mongol troops. Nor were the Europeans safe behind castle walls, for the Mongols were adept at siege warfare too. They

*A fourteenth-century Persian manuscript illustration shows Mongols in battle.*

learned from fighting Muslim armies how to build catapults for hurling rocks and burning pitch over city walls. In their conquest of northern China, the Mongols discovered how to make grenades out of gunpowder and clay.

Had not Ogodei died in December 1241, the Mongols might have overrun all of Europe. Instead, when news arrived of Ogodei's death, the Mongol leaders withdrew to Mongolia to choose Ogodei's successor as their great khan.

## CHRISTIAN ENVOYS TO THE MONGOLS

After the Mongols pulled back from eastern Europe in 1242, a new pope chose diplomacy over war. Eager to convert the Mongols to Christianity and form an alliance with them against Muslim rulers, the pope sent envoys with letters to Mongol leaders. One of these embassies, led by John of Plano Carpini, a Franciscan friar (a member of a religious order founded by St. Francis of Assisi in 1209), traveled all the way to the Mongolian capital at Karakorum (at the center of modern-day Mongolia) in 1246.

In a detailed report, Friar John wrote about the Mongol rulers and their history, the steppe (grassland) landscape of central Asia where they lived, and the people he met, as well as their customs and beliefs. These nomadic people herded horses, cattle, sheep, camels, and goats; hunted and foraged for other foods; and survived mainly on meat and milk. They lived in *gers*, round tents of felt that they could carry with them to different pastures for their herds, and wore clothing made from furs, leather, and felt. Although the Mongols had

# TATAR, TARTAR

Europeans at first confused the Mongols with the Tatars, one of the tribes Genghis Khan had conquered, and called them Tatars or, more often, Tartars. The added *r* was not accidental. To Europeans—especially between 1237 and 1241, when Ogodei's armies were attacking eastern Europe—this enemy seemed to come from Tartarus, the region of Hades in Greek mythology where wicked people suffered eternal torture after death. The name Tartar stuck. Polo used *Tartar*, not *Mongol*, throughout his book.

treated Friar John well, he found that the Mongols were not interested in becoming Christians. They had their own religion, worshipping the sky and Earth and holding the belief that spirits inhabited nature and that their priests, or shamans, had the ability to communicate with these spirits.

In 1253 King Louis IX of France sent another Franciscan friar, William of Rubruck, from the Crusader kingdom at Acre into the Mongol Empire to attempt conversion. Like Friar John before him, Friar William wrote a vivid account of his journey. His report provides one of the best sources of information about the Mongols in the mid-thirteenth century available today. His mission to convert the Mongols, however, was not successful either.

## THE MONGOL EMPIRE

The Mongols depended on settled people for grain, metals, and woven fabrics such as silk and cotton. To get these products, they either raided cities and towns or conquered them. After 1241 there were no further attacks on Europe because China and wealthy Islamic cities in what are modern Iran and Iraq promised far richer plunder and tribute than Europe.

Mongol troops captured the Muslim capital Baghdad in 1258. A grandson of Genghis Khan, Kublai, set out to overthrow the Song dynasty in southern China. Genghis Khan had granted Kublai's father control of large estates in northern China, so Kublai had lived much of his life there. In 1260 he was leading an army on the Chang River when he heard of the death of his brother, the most recent great khan. Without waiting for the traditional meeting to select a successor, Kublai declared himself the next great khan of the Mongols.

The empire Kublai took over was the largest in the world. It would grow larger, as Kublai was intent on defeating the Chinese Song

*Kublai Khan, grandson of Genghis Khan, ruled China in the thirteenth century. This painting was made about 1260.*

## THE FIRST EUROPEANS AT KUBLAI'S COURT?

Were Nicolo and Maffeo Polo really the first Europeans to meet Kublai Khan? According to one Chinese source, a group of foreigners visited Kublai Khan in June 1261. A diary kept by a Chinese official at Kublai's court describes them as blond and blue-eyed and says that they traveled across two seas to make their visit. It also says that they came from a country with constant daylight and no night. Perhaps they came from Novgorod in northern Russia or from Scandinavia (where the midsummer sun barely sets before rising) and crossed the Mediterranean and Black seas or the Black and Caspian seas on their journey to China. If so, they arrived before Nicolo and Maffeo Polo. Had the official only continued the diary—it ends in August 1261—perhaps he would have mentioned the Polo brothers as well.

dynasty, whose emperor was only a child. Mongol rule of China brought many changes to both the Mongol and the Chinese way of life.

## THE MONGOL EXPRESS

To speed communications within the empire, the Mongols built or repaired roads and canals. They planted trees, or in desert areas, they piled tall towers of stones along the roadsides to mark the way. The great khan's messengers galloped on swift horses along this network of roads. Every 25 miles (40 km), they reached a post house with fresh horses ready to go. In this way, Polo reports, "these messengers manage to cover 250 miles [400 km] a day with news for the Great Khan."

The most urgent messages traveled all night. If there was no moon, runners with torches lit the way, which slowed the pace but allowed messengers to cover 300 miles (480 km) in twenty-four hours. Such speed impressed Polo. In Europe traveling 100 miles (160 km) in a day was considered exceptionally fast.

Polo explains how the system functioned. Each city and town supplied and maintained the horses. They rotated half

*In this seventeenth-century manuscript painting, Wudi, a Chinese emperor of a later period, receives a letter delivered by the postal service that began operation before Marco Polo visited China.*

of the herd every month from the post stations to pastures so that rested and well-fed steeds were always available. At every large river or lake, the towns had several boats waiting to ferry messengers across. Towns on the edges of deserts had food and water ready for messengers to take with them.

The imperial postal service, called the *yamb* in Mongolian, also included foot runners who ran between stations 3 miles (5 km) apart carrying less pressing news or items. These runners wore belts with bells on them. The noise announced a runner's approach, so that the next runner could prepare to take over as soon as the first one reached his station. One of their jobs was keeping Kublai's summer palace at Shangdu (in what is modern Inner Mongolia, China) well supplied with fresh fruit from the winter capital of Khanbalik. They made the ten-day journey in a day and night.

Envoys and inspectors, Marco Polo among them, constantly traveled the well-kept roads to every province and to countries that promised to pay tribute in exchange for not being attacked. In this way, the great khan kept himself well informed about every corner of his empire.

## PAPER MONEY AND ECONOMIC CONTROL

As impressive as the postal system was, Polo was even more impressed by the money. He joked that the great khan had "mastered the art of alchemy," the trick of turning metals of little value into gold. Kublai's alchemy consisted of issuing paper money. Polo had never imagined that people would accept little rectangles of flattened mulberry bark stamped

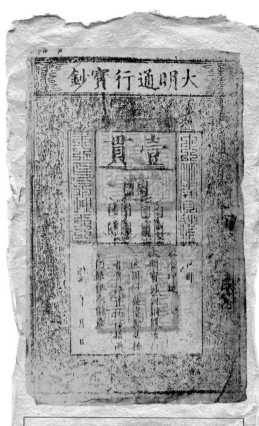

Marco Polo noted that Kublai Khan issued paper to be used as money— unheard of in Europe at the time. This is a photo of one of those bills.

with the khan's seal in the place of gold or silver coins, which were the currency of Europe. Kublai's subjects, however, had no choice. "No one dares refuse it," Polo said, "on pain of losing his life." By requiring all his subjects and foreign merchants to turn in their precious metals and gemstones for paper money, the great khan accumulated, Polo estimated, "more treasure than anyone else in the world."

Polo also noticed the measures Kublai took to assure a stable agricultural economy. In times of surplus, Kublai purchased crops to keep the price from falling too low. He stored the grain carefully to keep it from spoiling, building up a great supply of rice, millet, barley, and wheat. Then, in times of poor harvests, he distributed this grain so that everyone had enough to eat.

In spite of efforts by great khans to organize and unite the empire, by the 1260s, it was beginning to splinter.

Over the years, direct descendants of Genghis Khan had divided his realm into khanates, regions ruled by khans. In the northwest, the Khanate of the Golden Horde included much of modern Kazakhstan, southern Russia, and Ukraine. Its capital, Sarai, lay on the Volga River near the northern end of the Caspian Sea. In the southwest, the Ilkhanate (subordinate khanate) of Persia (Iran, Iraq, and part of Syria and Armenia) had its capital at Tabriz. The Chaghatai Khanate occupied central Asia (Tajikistan, Kyrgyzstan, Turkmenistan, and parts of Afghanistan, Uzbekistan, and western China). Kublai ruled directly in what are China, Mongolia, and Korea, although as great khan, in theory he ruled over the other khans as well.

## THE MONGOLS' RELIGIOUS TOLERANCE

The Mongol leader Kublai Khan regularly celebrated Christian feasts such as Christmas and Easter as well as the principal feasts of the Muslims, Jews, and Buddhists. When asked why, he replied: "There are four prophets who are worshipped and to whom all the world does reverence. The Christians say that their God was Jesus Christ, the Saracens Mahomet, the Jews Moses, and the idolaters Sakyamuni Burkhan [the Buddha], who was the first to be represented as God in the form of an idol. And I do honour and reverence to all four, so that I may be sure of doing it to him who is greatest in heaven and truest; and to him I pray for aid."

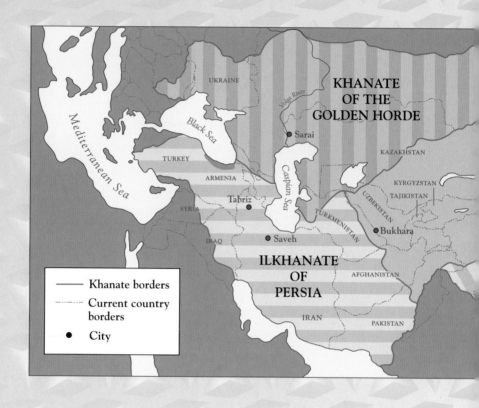

Border disputes and battles over the succession to the title of great khan often caused friction.

Even so, Mongol dominion over Asia brought together for the first time a huge expanse of territory under one overarching government. A passport from the great khan gave travelers safe access to the entire empire. The Mongols built roads and encouraged commerce and the exchange of ideas. Religious tolerance prevailed throughout the empire, although individual khans sometimes leaned toward or even adopted the religion of people they conquered. Berke Khan, who ruled the Golden Horde from 1257 to 1266, sympathized with Islam; Kublai, with Buddhism.

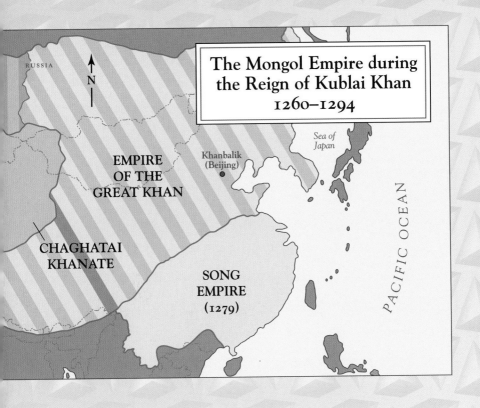

## The Mongol Empire during the Reign of Kublai Khan 1260–1294

RUSSIA

N

EMPIRE
OF THE
GREAT KHAN

Khanbalik
(Beijing)

Sea of
Japan

PACIFIC OCEAN

CHAGHATAI
KHANATE

SONG
EMPIRE
(1279)

As warlike as the Mongols were, they created a "Pax Mongolica"—a Mongol Peace—over a vast territory where warlords, bandits, and rulers hostile to foreigners once held sway. Among the first people from western Europe to take full advantage of the Mongol Peace were two Venetian brothers who set out from Constantinople in 1260 "in the hope of a profitable venture." They probably little imagined that they would travel across the entire continent and meet the great khan himself.

# CHAPTER THREE
# TRAVELING ACROSS ASIA

And in truth it makes one marvel to consider the immense extent of the journeys made, first by the Father and Uncle of the said Messer Marco, . . . all the way to the Court of the Great Can and the Emperor of the Tartars. . . . Consider only what a height of courage was needed to undertake and carry through so difficult an enterprise, over a route of such desperate length and hardship, whereon it was sometimes necessary to carry food for the supply of man and beast, not for days only but for months together.

—*Giovanni Battista Ramusio, Preface to* I Viaggi di Marco Polo *(The Voyages of Marco Polo), 1559*

While Marco Polo was growing up in Venice, his father and uncle embarked on a trip across Asia. Many Italian merchants traded in western Asia. But the Polo brothers were among the first Europeans to venture farther east. Friar John and Friar William had gone as far as Karakorum in Mongolia. The Polo brothers, it seems likely, crossed all the way to China.

After the French and Venetians conquered Constantinople in 1204, the Venetian doge crowned Baldwin of Flanders as the new emperor.

## A NEW TRADING VENTURE

The only source of information about Nicolo and Maffeo Polo's journey is the prologue to Marco Polo's book. According to that, the Polo brothers set out from Constantinople in 1260 to look for new markets. They may also have been fleeing political unrest. The government set up by the French and the Venetians in Constantinople was shaky. The Greeks who had formerly ruled there hoped to win back the city.

Nicolo and Maffeo put all their money into easy-to-carry jewels and sailed across the Black Sea to Sudak. It is possible that the Polo family already had the house there that the older Marco Polo mentioned in his will twenty years later in 1280.

Sudak was a major port at the time. Friar William reported that traders from Russia brought "squirrel and ermine and other valuable furs" to Sudak to exchange for "cotton . . . , silk stuffs and sweet-smelling spices" shipped across the Black Sea from what is now northern Turkey.

From Sudak the Polos set out on their adventure to eastern lands. Marco Polo's book does not say how they traveled. When Friar William made the journey a few years earlier, he and his four companions had the choice of riding on horseback or traveling in covered oxcarts. Not wanting to unload and reload horses at every stop, the friar chose the carts. The carts also gave the small group a place to sleep on the journey, for they saw few towns along the way.

Like Friar William, the Polo brothers probably took an interpreter with them and a slave boy to help cook and set up camp each night. They also must have taken small gifts to buy the goodwill of officials or local chieftains. A group of men on horseback surrounded Friar William's cart as it entered Mongol territories and demanded food and drink from the travelers. They also wanted their knives, gloves, purses, and belts—whatever struck their fancy. The Polo brothers probably faced similar demands.

Traveling north and east, through the hilly landscape of southern Ukraine into Russia, the Polo brothers came to the court of Berke, khan of the Golden Horde, near the Volga River. Based on Friar William's account, the trip would have taken the Polos about a month by horseback or two months by oxcart.

On arriving, Nicolo and Maffeo gave all their jewels to the khan. Berke, in exchange, gave them goods to trade.

The book reports that the goods were worth twice the value of the jewels. In this way, Mongol leaders encouraged commerce while acquiring useful treasure for themselves. The Polo brothers remained in Berke's land for a year.

## INTO CENTRAL ASIA

In 1261 a civil war broke out between Berke Khan and his cousin Hulagu, ilkhan of Persia. When Hulagu won a major victory, the Polos feared for their safety. It seemed wiser to move farther east than to attempt to retreat through the lands disputed in the war. Marco Polo's book does not mention that the same year, Constantinople returned to Greek rule. Venetian traders would not be safe there either.

"Since we cannot return to Constantinople with our wares," the book reports that the brothers said to each other, "let us go on towards the east. Then we can come back by a roundabout route."

Crossing the Volga River and traveling around the northern end of the Caspian Sea, the Polo brothers, traversed the dry steppes of Kazakhstan and Uzbekistan to the ancient city of Bukhara. The Mongols had captured and destroyed the city in 1220. When the Polos arrived, it was one of the chief cities of the Chaghatai Khanate.

The brothers stayed in Bukhara for three years, waiting for the unrest in the western khanates to end. It must have been an uneasy three years, but it may have given the Polos a chance to learn the Mongol language. Perhaps they also still had goods to sell in the city, which was an important stop along the east-west overland trade routes.

# MEETING THE GREAT KHAN

In 1265 an envoy from Hulagu came through Bukhara on his way to the Great Khan Kublai. Surprised to meet "Latins" (Europeans) in the city, the envoy insisted that they come with him to the great khan's court. "Sirs," Polo's book reports the envoy as saying, "I assure you that the Great Khan of the Tartars has never seen any Latin and is exceedingly desirous to meet one. Therefore, if you accompany me to him, I assure you that he will be very glad to see you and will treat you with great honour and great bounty. And you will be able to travel with me in safety without let or hindrance."

The journey, the prologue says, took a year. It does not reveal the precise route, only saying that they rode "towards the north and the northeast." Nor does it say exactly where Kublai Khan was holding court when they got there. They may have been at the summer palace at Shangdu, at the new capital that Kublai was building in Khanbalik, or at one of Kublai Khan's great traveling camps.

Kublai Khan welcomed the brothers and peppered them with questions about Europe, its leaders, and its customs. He asked the brothers to take a letter to the pope in Rome with a request for one hundred learned men. He was probably not interested in having them convert his subjects to Christianity. More likely, he wanted educated Europeans to help run his empire.

Kublai also asked for some holy oil from the lamp that burns in the Church of the Holy Sepulcher in Jerusalem, a church built on the site of Christ's tomb. This oil, people believed, could cure diseases. Kublai had perhaps heard of this.

ou estoit le seigneur. Et deuauchant trouuant moult de grans merueilles
et de dauersitez, de choses lesquelles nous ne conterons pas ore. Pour ce que le g
messire marc pol qui toutes ces choses vist. aussy le vous contera en cest liure
en auant tout apertement.

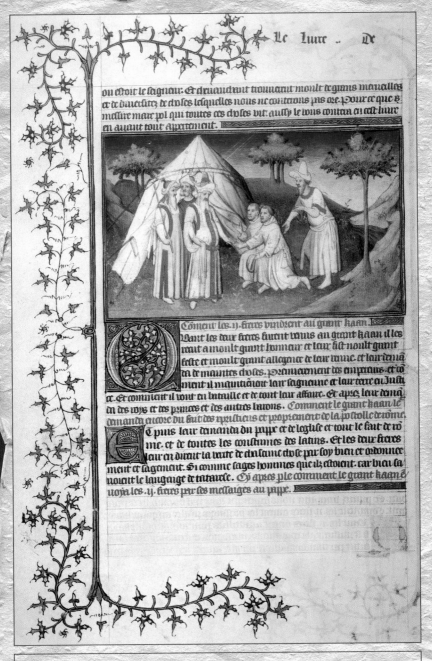

Coment les ij. freres vindrent au grant kaan.

Quant les deur freres furent venus au grant kaan il les
vint a moult grant honnour et leur fist moult grant
feste et moult grant allegrice de leur venue. et leur dema
da de maintes choses. Premierement des empereurs. et co
ment il maintindrent leur seigneurie et leur terre en iustic
ce. Et comment il vont en bataille et de tout leur affaire. Et apres. leur dema
da des roys et des princes et des autres barons. Comment le grant kaan le
demanda encore du fait des esglises et proprement de la posteille de romme.
Epuis leur demanda du pappe et de leglise et tout le fait de ro
me. et de toutes les coustumes des latins. Et les deur freres
leur en dirent la verite de chascune chose par soy bien et ordonnee
ment et sagement. Si comme sages hommes que ilz estoient. car bien sa
uoient le langaige de tartarie. Et apres pie comment le grant kaan e
uoya les ij. freres par ses messaiges au pappe.

---

*The Polo brothers are welcomed by Kublai Khan in front of his tent
in this illustration from a fifteenth-century French manuscript.*

To ease the Polos' way, Kublai gave them a tablet of gold. The writing on this tablet gave the travelers the right to lodging, horses, and escorts through all the lands of the Mongol Empire. But it did not make their return journey very fast. According to the prologue, it took three years, "because they could not ride all the time, but were delayed by stress of weather, by snow and by swollen rivers." One historian suggests that Polo exaggerated the length of the journey to make China seem even farther away than it is. The book says nothing of the route they took.

In April 1269, the Polo brothers reached Acre. Here they learned that the pope had died. According to the book, a papal legate, or representative of the pope, in Acre advised them to wait for the election of a new pope. In the book, the papal legate is referred to as Teobaldo Visconti. But Teobaldo was not a papal legate nor was he in Acre at that time. This mistake is not surprising. Polo's son was working from memory of things he heard about thirty years earlier.

Nicolo and Maffeo sailed from Acre to Venice "to see their families" while they waited to deliver their letter from Kublai Khan to the new pope. The fifteen-year-old Marco must have been excited to see his father and his uncle, especially if (as one source says) it was the first time he had ever seen his father.

## MARCO SETS OUT

The time it took to elect the next pope—almost three years—was one of the longest papal elections in history. The Polo brothers grew impatient. Would the khan think badly

# A USEFUL PASSPORT

Kublai Khan issued metal tablets of command, often called *paizi* (from the Chinese word for "plaques"), to officials in his government. These tablets could be made of iron, silver, or gold and took a variety of shapes. Some were symbols of the office to which the receiver was assigned. Others were passports for important guests or people on state missions. They entitled Kublai's ambassadors to horses, lodging, and guides provided by the imperial postal system. A Mongol tablet of command that can be seen at the Metropolitan Museum of Art in New York City has written on it, "By the strength of Eternal Heaven, an edict of the Emperor [Khan]. He who has no respect shall be guilty."

of them for taking so long? But for young Marco, the delay was probably an advantage. By 1271, when the Polo brothers gave up waiting, Marco was seventeen years old, certainly old enough to go along on the return journey to Kublai Khan.

They set out in the summer of 1271, young Marco with them. First, they sailed to Acre in the Holy Land. The walled city facing the sea was crowded with Crusaders planning a campaign to regain Jerusalem. Leading the Crusade was Prince Edward of England, who was soon to become the next English king. Traveling with him was the archbishop of Liège (in what is today Belgium), Teobaldo Visconti—the man Marco later mistakenly remembered as having advised his father and uncle two years earlier.

Teobaldo arranged for the Polos to go to Jerusalem to get the oil that Kublai Khan had requested. In spite of impending warfare with the Crusaders, the Muslim rulers of Jerusalem allowed Christian pilgrims to visit the Holy City. Teobaldo also gave the Polos letters for the great khan explaining that there was no pope who could send the learned men the khan requested.

The Polos sailed to Ayas, now a small village on the southern coast of Turkey but at the time one of the busiest ports for Venice's Asian trade. Here word caught up with them that Teobaldo had been chosen pope. The Polos

This image shows the Polos leaving Venice to begin their journey to China. It is from a fourteenth-century manuscript in the Bodleian Library at Oxford, England.

returned to Acre to see the new pope, who took the name Gregory X. The pope chose two friars—in place of the one hundred men the khan had asked for—to accompany the Polos on their journey and sent many fine gifts as well.

The two friars, the book says, were "the wisest in all that province." But neither was ready for the risks of traveling beyond Christendom. After sailing back to Ayas, the small group was preparing to travel inland when they heard that the sultan of Egypt planned to attack Armenia. Frightened for their safety, the friars quickly arranged to return to Acre.

## A "DESCRIPTION OF THE WORLD," NOT A TRAVEL BOOK

The prologue to Marco Polo's book provides only a teaser about what happened on the rest of the journey to China: "So Messer Niccolò [another spelling of Marco's father's name] and Messer Maffeo and Marco, the son of Niccolò, set out on their journey and rode on, winter and summer, till they came to the Great Khan. . . . What they saw on the way will not be mentioned here, because we will recount it to you later in our book, all in due order. Here you need only know that they were hard put to it to complete the journey in three and a half years, because of snow and rain and flooded rivers and because they could not ride in winter as well as in summer."

After the prologue ends with the return of the Polos to Venice in 1295, however, the tone of the book changes. The first chapter opens with: "Let me begin with Armenia. The truth is that there are actually two Armenias, a Greater and a Lesser." We are no longer reading a story about three

# A MIRACLE LAMP

A pilgrim who visited the Church of the Holy Sepulcher before the Polos wrote that the lamp there had miraculously remained lit since Christ was placed in the tomb: "The Lamp which had been placed by [Christ's] head (when He lay there) still burns on the same spot day and night." Like the Polos, this pilgrim also "took a blessing from it"—he took a small amount of the oil as a charm to avert evil or bring good fortune.

Venetian merchants traveling toward China, but a geography book.

Marco Polo's name, for example, first appears a dozen pages later in a description of the Persian city of Saveh (in northwestern Iran), where "Messer Marco asked several of the inhabitants" about three tombs in that city. The travelers are mentioned from time to time, but the focus remains on the information Marco Polo gathered, revealing little about their route and their adventures along the way.

## RECONSTRUCTING THE ROUTE

The descriptions in the book begin with places in western Asia and move east. Many places described, however, lie north or south of the major east-west trade routes of the time. No one thinks that Polo visited all these areas. It seems likely that the Polos went through Saveh because Marco writes of having questioned the city's inhabitants.

But even that is not certain. It is always possible that Polo met travelers from Saveh who told him about the tombs of the three Magi who visited the Christ child. As the prologue points out, "There is also much here that he has not seen but has heard from men of credit and veracity."

To figure out the Polos' itinerary, historians pore over different manuscripts of *The Travels*, consult maps, and read the accounts of other travelers. Some Polo fans even travel to Asia to test their theories.

Details vary, but historians generally agree that the Polos traveled overland across what is now Turkey, Iran, northern Afghanistan, and the People's Republic of China. Even today the territory they covered is daunting. In a journey of more than 7,500 miles (12,000 km), they traveled across a challenging landscape of deserts, high mountain passes, and salt flats that covered treacherous mud bogs.

Robbers were also a danger. In desolate areas, they waylaid travelers during sandstorms, seizing livestock and people to sell as slaves. "Messer Marco himself narrowly evaded capture" in such an attack, the book reports.

The journey perhaps began on horseback. As the Polos moved toward the drier areas of central Asia, however, they must have exchanged their mounts, since horses cannot travel far without water. Most likely, they rode on "ships of the desert"—hardy, two-humped Bactrian camels. Camels can go without water for several days because they can tolerate very high body temperatures and perspire very little. Or the Polos may have ridden the tough little donkeys that Polo mentions as costing even more than horses. For safety, they probably joined other travelers in a caravan.

Genoa

Venice

POLAND

EUROPE

Rome

ITALY

Zara
(Zadar)

HUNGARY

Kiev

Moscow

RUSSIA

Volga River

ALBANIA

BULGARIA

UKRAINE

GREECE

DALMATIAN COAST

Black
Sea

Soldaia

Sarai

KAZAKHSTAN

Mediterranean Sea

Constantinople

TURKEY

ARMENIA

Trebizond

UZBEKISTAN

KYRGYZSTAN

Ayaz

Caspian Sea

Samarkand

TAJIKISTAN

Alexandria

SYRIA

MOUNT
ARARAT

Tabriz

Bukhara

Tyre

Mosul

Haifa

Tigris
River

TURKMENISTAN

Acre

Jerusalem

PERSIA

Baghdad

Saveh

Sheberghan

PAMIR
MOUNTAINS

EGYPT

IRAQ

IRAN

Balkh

Kashgar

Euphrates
River

AFGHANISTAN

Amu
Darya
River

Red Sea

Persian Gulf

Kerman

PAKISTAN

AFRICA

Hormuz

Arabian Sea

INDIA

INDIAN
OCEAN

Possible route
of Marco Polo

Possible route
of the elder Polos

Grand Canal

Current country
border

City

Hubei Province

SRI
LANKA

## Marco Polo's Travels
### 1271–1295

N

ASIA

MONGOLIA

Karakorum

Shangdu

Khanbalik
(Beijing)

JAPAN

GANSU

HEBEI

KOREA

East
China
Sea

TAKLIMAKAN
(DESERT OF LOP)

SHANXI

CHINA

Sa-chau
(Dunhuang)

SHAANXI

JIANGSU

Yangzhou

KUNLUN
MOUNTAINS

Huang River

Xianyang

ANHUI

Hangzhou

ZHEJIANG

TIBET

SICHUAN

Chang River

HUBEI

PACIFIC OCEAN

FUJIAN

Yunnan

Quanzhou

YUNNAN

MYANMAR
(BURMA)

LAOS

SOUTHEAST ASIA

VIETNAM

THAILAND
(SIAM)

Andaman
Islands

SUMATRA

This drawing on a Catalan (part of Spain) world map from 1375 is thought to represent Nicolo and Maffeo Polo and their Mongol escorts traveling through central Asia.

Hundreds of animals with riders or pack loads formed a well-organized procession that trotted along at about 3 miles (5 km) an hour.

## ACROSS CENTRAL ASIA

From Ayas it seems that the Polos traveled through Turkish villages of mud brick houses, blue-domed mosques, and tall minarets, treeless scrubland where sheep and goats foraged for food, and stretches of green farmland in river valleys. Along the way, inns called caravansaries provided shelter for travelers and their animals. Near the border with Iran, the

Polos may have seen the snowcapped peak of Mount Ararat, where the Bible says Noah's ark landed.

It is likely that the Polos stopped in Tabriz, in what is now northwestern Iran. After Hulagu destroyed Baghdad in 1258, Tabriz had become his capital and a major center for trade between the Persian Gulf region and the Mediterranean. The Polos must have met other Italian merchants bringing wares to this important city to trade for precious stones from India and the cloth of silk and gold woven locally.

From Tabriz they traveled in a southeasterly direction across the dry plains of central Iran toward the city of Kerman. Along the way, they stopped at or passed near Saveh. In Kerman, Polo noted the turquoises, steel weapons, fine embroideries, and falcons for hunting.

The Polos may have tired of land travel and hoped to catch a ship to hasten the journey to China. Instead of moving east from Kerman, the description turns south toward Hormuz, a seaport in modern-day Iran at the entrance to the Persian Gulf. Although the markets of Hormuz impressed Polo, the ships did not. With only wooden pegs and thread made from coconut husks holding them together, the book says, it is "a risky undertaking to sail in these ships."

After the side trip to Hormuz, the Polos headed north and east. They crossed deserts of "utter drought" where "neither fruit nor trees" grew and oases with "rich herbage, fine pasturage, fruit in plenty, and no lack of anything." Their route seems to have crossed into northern Afghanistan. Details about the sliced melons set out to dry in the sun in Sheberghan and about the rubble of Balkh, a city destroyed by Genghis Khan in 1222, sound like eyewitness reports. The Polos then followed part of the Amu Darya River toward its source in the Pamir Mountain highlands of northeastern Afghanistan.

The book mentions that the healthy mountain air heals fevers and reports that "Messer Marco vouches for this from his own experience." Historians have suggested that he caught malaria in Hormuz, which he described as "torrid" and "unhealthy," and recovered his health in the Pamirs.

The trail through the mountain passes in the Pamirs reaches 15,000 feet (4,600 m). The Polos must have crossed it in the summer, since for half the year, it is "snow-filled and impenetrable." Polo noticed the effect of the altitude on the time it took to cook food. Because liquids boil at lower temperatures where there is less air pressure—as at high altitudes—cooking food takes longer than at sea level. Polo, however, thought it was because of the cold that "food does not cook well" in the mountains. The long, rugged journey, "always over mountains and along hillsides and gorges, traversing many rivers and many deserts," at last led down from the Pamirs into what is now western China.

## INTO CHINA

The Polos still had more than 2,600 miles (4,200 km) to go before they would reach the court of Kublai Khan. They found fertile farmlands with orchards, vineyards, and fields of cotton, hemp, and flax in the valleys below the Kunlun Mountains of western China, where snowmelt provided irrigation. But a vast desert lay in their eastward path.

# THE ROOF OF THE WORLD

The Pamirs are one of six major mountain chains in central Asia.
All of these ranges rise above 24,000 feet (7,300 m). Together
they boast the sixty-seven tallest peaks in the world. The
shortest of the six ranges, the Pamirs form a knot from which the
other five extend. The Hindu Kush leads to the west; the
Himalayas, the Karakorum, and the Kunlun Shan to the
southeast, and the Tian Shan to the northeast. The highest
Pamir peaks are in Tajikistan, and parts of the chain cross into
northeastern Afghanistan, northern India, and western China.
The name *Pamir* is Persian for "the roof of the world."

The name of the desert, *Taklimakan*, means "go in and you won't come out."

Polo calls it the Desert of Lop, for Lop is the town where they stopped for a week to prepare for the arduous journey. Packing a month's supply of food for themselves and their animals, they set out, most likely on camels and with a guide to lead them to the desert oases, where they could find food and water. Polo does not mention the shifting sand dunes, tall as mountains, that whisper in travelers' ears. To him the strange sounds made by the wind on the sand were the voices of spirits. Travelers must be wary, he says, of letting these voices lead them astray.

*Travelers still cross the Taklimakan Desert of western China in camel caravans, just as they did in Marco Polo's time.*

# MARCO POLO'S SHEEP

In writing about the Pamirs, Polo described "great quantities of wild sheep," huge animals with horns "as much as six palms [57 to 60 inches (145 to 152 cm)] in length." Shepherds, he said, used the horns to craft large bowls and to make pens for their flocks. The scientific name given later to these sheep is *Ovis ammon polii*, the *polii* in honor of Marco Polo. These sheep are an endangered species.

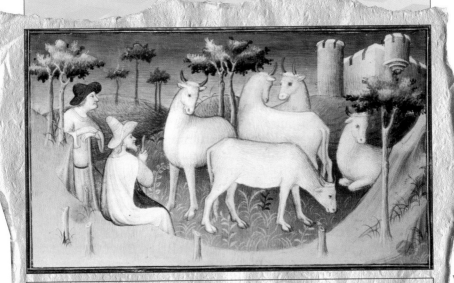

This drawing of Marco Polo's sheep is from a fifteenth-century French manuscript.

"For this reason," his book points out, "bands of travellers make a point of keeping very close together. Before they go to sleep they set up a sign pointing in the direction in which they have to travel. And round the necks of all their beasts they fasten little bells, so that by listening to the sound they may prevent them from straying off the path."

Once across the desert, the Polos reached the province of Gansu in central China, called Tangut in Polo's book. For the first time in their journey, they were among Chinese people. They likely stopped at Dunhuang, which Polo calls

*An eighth-century banner from Dunhuang, a likely stop on Marco Polo's journey, shows Buddha preaching.*

Sa-chau. Dunhuang was a hub of east-west and north-south trade routes and a center of Buddhist worship. Polo noticed "many abbeys and monasteries, all full of idols of various forms to which they make sacrifices and do great honour and reverence."

As the book begins to describe cities and people of China, it is difficult to be certain which cities they traveled through on their way to Kublai Khan's court. The prologue, however, says that when they were still forty days' journey away, couriers from Kublai Khan met them. They escorted the three Venetians to Kublai's summer palace in Shangdu.

The Polos had at last arrived. The trek had taken three and a half years.

# CHAPTER FOUR
# MARCO POLO IN CHINA

Messer Marco observed more of the peculiarities of this part of the world than any other man, because he travelled more widely in these outlandish regions than any man who was ever born, and also because he gave his mind more intently to observing them.

—*Marco Polo*, The Travels, *1299*

The historic meeting between Marco Polo and the great khan probably took place during the summer of 1275. Kublai Khan was fifty-nine years old, Marco just twenty-one. At Shangdu, the book reports, "Kublai Khan built a huge palace of marble and other ornamental stones. Its halls and chambers are all gilded, and the whole building is marvellously embellished and richly adorned." Two manuscripts report rooms and passages that were "wonderfully painted within

Kublai Khan's new summer palace may have looked like this one in an early Chinese painting on silk.

with pictures and images of beasts and birds and trees and flowers and many kinds of things, so well and so cunningly that it is a delight and a wonder to see."

The palace no longer exists, but foundations for it measure a grandiose 75,000 square feet (7,000 sq. m), about the size of a modern football stadium. The only other signs of its grandeur are the broken bits of marble and glazed tiles that modern archaeologists found on the grassy site.

## KUBLAI KHAN WELCOMES THE POLOS

According to the prologue to Marco Polo's book, the great khan was seated with "a very great company of barons" around him. The Polos "knelt before him and made obeisance with the

*Marco Polo is introduced to Kublai Khan. His father and uncle are dressed as friars in this manuscript painting from a copy of Jean de Mandeville's* Book of Marvels, *which dates to the fourteenth century. The artist misunderstood the text.*

utmost humility. The Great Khan bade them rise and received them honourably and entertained them with great cheer."

The words give only a general idea of the scene. Marco Polo apparently stood aside as the great khan greeted his father and uncle. When the khan received the letters from the pope and the holy oil, he was "greatly pleased" and even joyful, the book reports. Only then did the khan notice the young man and ask who he was.

"'Sire,' Nicolo replied, 'he is my son and your liege man.' 'He is heartily welcome,' said the Khan."

## THE KHAN'S LIEGE MAN

Nicolo Polo says that Marco is "*vestre home*," or "your man." In Europe at that time, for a nobleman to become someone's man meant that he swore allegiance to the higher-ranked lord or a king. He became his liege man, offering his military services in exchange for land. The Mongols organized their military with similar vows of service and rewards of land.

Nicolo Polo, however, was not offering his son to the Mongol army. He was promising Marco's loyalty and readiness to serve the khan. The Polos had come to China not as merchants but as diplomats. Kublai had sent them to the pope, and the pope had sent them back. The book does not state their exact mission. Rather, the purpose of their journey seems to have been to establish a line of communication between Europe and Mongol China. The pope and the Polos wanted to further Christianity in China, to maintain peaceful ties, and to promote trade.

Kublai Khan probably saw

This woodcut illustration of Marco as a young man appears in the first printed edition of Marco Polo's book. It was published in Nuremberg, Germany, in 1477.

potential in the young man at that first meeting. His court was full of non-Mongols—Chinese, Tibetan, Persian—whom he trusted as advisers and envoys. We do not know what Marco Polo looked like. No portrait made during his lifetime exists, and descriptions of him only speak generally of his honesty, piety, prudence, and respectability. His book, however, shines with energy, intelligence, and curiosity. Most likely, Kublai Khan saw these qualities at once. It was not long before he decided how to use the young Venetian's talents.

## KUBLAI'S INTEREST IN THE POLOS

If the khan was disappointed that the Polos had returned without the one hundred educated men he had asked for, the book does not say so. Instead, Kublai "entertained them with good cheer." It is possible that Polo was exaggerating his importance to this renowned ruler, but it is also possible that Kublai was genuinely interested in the Venetian merchants.

Kublai Khan had several reasons for such interest. As an outsider, a Mongol ruling China, Kublai constantly needed to make his reign appear legitimate. To have visitors come from lands as far away as Italy would enhance Kublai Khan's status among his Chinese subjects.

The Polos also brought to Kublai's court a gold mine of information about Europe. Neither the Mongols nor the Chinese knew very much about lands to the west. Just as Europeans imagined strange beings and fabulous riches in the East, eastern Asians developed their own myths about Western peoples. Far to the west, they believed, lay an enchanted land of blue-eyed giants.

# THE YUAN DYNASTY

When his brother the great khan died, Kublai declared himself not only the great khan of the Mongols but also the emperor of China. He later took the name for his new dynasty, Yuan, from an ancient Chinese philosophical work, *The Book of Changes*. In this book, the phrase *Ch'ien Yuan* means "the original creative force."

To win the support of the Chinese people, Kublai adopted many Chinese customs. He patterned his government on Chinese models and built his capital in the Chinese style, giving it the Chinese name Da-du (Great Capital). He chose Chinese architecture for the city's temples and palaces and decorated them with phoenixes and dragons. At court he used Chinese rituals, accompanied by Chinese music, and even gave the son he hoped would succeed him a Chinese name and education. (The prince died, however, nine years before his father.)

Kublai's grandson Temur reigned successfully for thirteen years after Kublai's death in 1294, but his successors were weak rulers, many of whom died young from excessive drinking. By the mid-fourteenth century, Mongol rule in China was losing ground to Chinese rebels. In 1368 the son of a poor farmworker chased the last Mongol emperor out of Da-du and established himself as the emperor of the new Ming ("Brilliant" or "Glorious") dynasty.

A divine queen ruled this mountain paradise, where drinking a holy elixir could make a person immortal.

In the early thirteenth century, a Chinese official named Chau Ju-kua collected more reliable information about lands west of China from Muslim traders who came to the port of Zaiton on the east coast of China. His *Description of the Barbarian Peoples*, however, only carried information about Islamic countries, which in Europe included only southern Spain and Sicily. The Polos could tell Kublai about Christian Europe.

The letters from the pope added to the Polos' value. Through visiting missionaries, the Mongols knew the pope was an important European leader and that European Christians were at war with the Muslim rulers of Egypt and Syria over the Holy Land. The Mongols were themselves fighting against the same Muslim forces, who were trying to win back lands the Mongols had seized as they expanded their empire. Kublai Khan was eager to keep open the possibility that Christians and Mongols would join forces against the Muslims.

Kublai also had a keen interest in science and technology. At the time, China and Islamic lands were more advanced in these areas than Europe, but Kublai Khan may not have known that. He had learned a great deal about farming, finance, and firearms from the Chinese and the Muslims. He no doubt hoped to discover useful things from the well-traveled Venetians as well.

Polo boasts that he made it possible for the Mongols to end the long siege of Xiangyang during Kublai's war against the Song emperor. According to his book, the Polos told

Kublai Khan about two men traveling with them—Polo does not say who they were or whether they were guides, interpreters, servants, or even other travelers they had met on their long journey. These men knew how to build powerful siege engine catapults and agreed to build some for the Mongols. When these machines began hurling 300-pound (135 kg) stones into the Chinese city, the people quickly surrendered. Other sources say that two Muslim engineers from central Asia built the catapults. The battle mentioned in the book took place in 1273, two years before the Polos arrived at Kublai's court. So most historians agree that Polo's account is mistaken.

Finally, Kublai wanted to encourage trade. It helped unite his vast empire, provided work and goods for his subjects, and enriched the imperial treasury. Kublai no doubt

This diagram shows a type of siege engine catapult developed in Europe in the Middle Ages.

viewed the Polos' marketing skills favorably and listened to their ideas about trade.

## SERVING THE KHAN

The khan accepted the Polos as honored guests. "They stayed at court," the prologue says, "and had a place of honour above the other barons." Polo uses the European term *barons* to refer to the members of Kublai's family who held important positions in his government as well as to his chief advisers and civil servants, most of whom were not Mongols.

The book says little about how Nicolo and Maffeo spent their time. Some historians speculate that they engaged in trade. Marco, the prologue says, set to work perfecting his knowledge of four languages and how they were written. During the three and a half years' journey, he no doubt started learning Persian, Turkish, and Mongolian. No one knows which his fourth language was, perhaps Arabic or Tibetan. It does not seem to have been Chinese.

Before long, the khan selected Marco to go as his envoy to Kara-jang, the modern-day province of Yunnan. Bordering on Myanmar, Laos, and Vietnam, Yunnan is about 1,500 miles (2,500 km) southwest of the Chinese capital in Beijing. The book does not explain what his business was, only that it took him a good six months to get there.

The young Marco had already noticed how other envoys did their work. When they returned to Kublai's court with only information concerning their specific mission, Kublai "would call them dolts and dunces" because "he would rather hear reports of these strange countries, and of their customs and usages, than the business on which he had sent them." So when Marco traveled, "he paid close attention to all the novelties and curiosities that came his way."

On his return, Marco "presented himself before the Khan and first gave a full account of the business on which he was sent—he had accomplished it very well. Then he went on to recount all the remarkable things he had seen on the way, so well and shrewdly that the Khan, and all those who heard him, were amazed and said to one another: 'If this youth lives to manhood, he cannot fail to prove himself a man of sound judgement and true worth.'"

*The Polos and Kublai Khan atop four elephants are part of a hunting party in this French painting. It is from a manuscript version of Marco Polo's book that dates to about 1410.*

The customs of different peoples clearly fascinated both men. Marco's curiosity and keen eye for detail impressed Kublai. For carrying out this first assignment so well, Kublai apparently gave Marco a title. The book uses the French equivalent of Sir, reporting that "from this time onwards the young fellow was called Messer Marco Polo."

One historian suggests that Polo supervised the salt trade in Yangzhou, a city on the Grand Canal in eastern China. Polo says that he governed this city for three years, but no Chinese sources support this claim. Perhaps, the historian proposes, Polo considered that running the state monopoly on salt made him the real governor of Yangzhou.

During the seventeen years that the Polos remained in China, Messer Marco traveled extensively. As he carried out the business assigned to him, he gathered information for the great khan. He must have already been planning to bring all that he learned back to Europe as well.

## A SIZABLE EMPIRE

In the middle third of his book, Polo describes China. For a European, Mongol China was nothing short of amazing. The sheer size of the territory that Kublai controlled directly was astounding. Besides ruling almost all of modern China, Mongolia, and Korea, after 1287 Kublai received tribute from large parts of what are now Vietnam and Myanmar.

The military force needed to occupy such a vast empire impressed Polo. He admired the way the Mongols organized their armies and noted how efficiently they traveled.

# FROM CHINA TO EUROPE

The first person from China known to have traveled in Europe arrived in Naples, Italy, in 1287, when Marco Polo, his father, and his uncle were living in China. Bar Sauma was a Christian monk of Turkish descent who was born and raised in China. About ten years before he arrived in Europe, he left China and settled for a time in Persia.

In 1286 the Mongol ruler of Persia, Arghun (who is mentioned in Polo's book), sent a delegation to Europe to seek help in defeating the Muslim rulers in Syria and the Holy Land. He chose Sauma to head the mission because he was Christian, fluent in several languages, and had traveled widely.

On his journey, Sauma met King Philip IV of France in Paris and King Edward I of England in Bordeaux, in southwestern France, which then belonged to England. He spent a winter in Genoa while waiting for the election of Pope Nicholas IV. Everywhere he went, he visited churches and shrines, admiring the many Christian relics on display. He kept a diary of his travels, recording, for instance, the eruption of Mount Etna as his ship passed Sicily.

In the end, Sauma's mission failed its purpose. The kings were eager to undertake a new Crusade with Mongol help, but the pope was not. After a year in Europe, Sauma returned to Persia. Had he succeeded in gaining papal support, his journey, like Polo's, might have marked a pivotal moment in world history.

Mongol warriors show off their horsemanship to impress the Chinese.

Each man had his own supplies and spare horses, so that the army could move swiftly. European armies, by contrast, were slowed by baggage trains. He praised the stamina of Mongol warriors as well as their horsemanship and their skillful maneuvering in battle.

With his huge military force, Kublai stationed large numbers of Mongol troops throughout his dominion to forestall any uprisings by his Chinese subjects. City gates and walls, Polo observed, had been torn down. That way, the army could easily enter to put down a revolt. The great khan also had to defend his position from other Mongols who hoped to replace him. Kublai sent armies to expand his empire as well, although two attempts to invade Japan and one to conquer Java (an island of Indonesia) failed.

To run his government, Kublai required a well-organized civil service. Like the "twelve great and powerful barons" who supervised all decisions concerning the armies, another twelve barons had authority over the thirty-four provinces of Kublai's empire. They appointed governors, with the great khan's approval, oversaw the collection of taxes, and distributed government funds.

## POLO'S TRAVELS IN CHINA

Polo organized his descriptions of places in China along two travel routes. One itinerary led southwest from Khanbalik over mountains and down river valleys through the modern provinces of Hebei, Shanxi, Shaanxi, and Sichuan to Yunnan and the Myanmar border. The other headed south and east from Khanbalik into the fertile plains of eastern China, with its thickly settled towns and cities, across the modern provinces of Hebei, Shandong, Anhui, Jiangsu, and Zhejiang to Fujian on the southeastern coast.

In other parts of the book, Polo wrote about places in western Asia that he did not see personally, such as Baghdad, Mosul, Samarkand, and Karakorum. In writing about China, however, he took a different approach. Mentioning the Huang River on the second route, he noted that "when you cross this river" you are leaving Cathay (northern China) and entering Manzi (southern China). "But," he added, "you must not suppose that we have dealt exhaustively with the whole province of Cathay, or indeed with the twentieth part of it. Only such cities have been described as I, Marco, passed through on my journey through the province, leaving out those on either side and the intervening regions whose enumerations would be too tedious."

# A WELL-ORGANIZED, EFFICIENT, AND OBEDIENT WAR MACHINE

Polo admired the military organization of the Mongols, which he explained as follows:

When a lord of the Tartars goes out to war with a following of 100,000 horsemen, he has . . . one captain in command of every ten, one of every one hundred, one of every thousand and one of every ten-thousand, so that he never needs to consult with more than ten men. In the same way each commander of ten-thousand or a thousand or a hundred consults only with his ten immediate subordinates, and each man is answerable to his own chief. When the supreme commander wishes to send someone on an operation, he orders the commander of ten-thousand to give him a thousand men; the latter orders the captain of a thousand to contribute his share. So the order is passed down, each commander being required to furnish his quota toward the thousand. At each stage it is promptly received and executed. For they are all obedient to the word of command more than any other people in the world.

Polo likely traveled on these routes or parts of them more than once during his years in China. He also wrote about commuting seasonally between the khan's two capitals and going on hunting trips with the khan's court to a seaside area east of Khanbalik. In addition, he made at least one sea voyage. According to the prologue, toward the end of his stay, Polo "returned from India by a voyage over strange seas."

Among the sights in China that impressed Polo most were the many large cities of eastern China and the busy, boat-filled rivers and canals linking them together. Traveling southeast from Khanbalik, he remarked, are "cities and

*Marco, Nicolo, and Maffeo Polo visit a port on the Huang (Yellow) River. This illustration is from a fourteenth-century French manuscript of Marco Polo's book.*

towns in plenty all the way, centres of thriving trade and industry." But he also liked to describe smaller, out-of-the-way places and curiosities he came across on his journeys.

## PRODUCTS, BEASTS, AND PEOPLES OF CHINA

As Polo traveled on the great khan's business, he noted the products of each area he passed through. The book points out the availability of salt, many kinds of silk fabrics, gold, turquoise, pearls, rhubarb, musk, cloves, ginger, cinnamon, and cotton. At times Polo estimates the value of these goods.

*Marco was impressed by the busy river and canal traffic linking Chinese cities. This scene of boats on a river was painted on silk in China about the time Marco Polo visited.*

Polo also wrote about fish, birds, game, farm animals, such as pigs and chickens, and wild animals, such as tigers and jackals. He described bamboo canes and the little white flowers of the clove tree. But most of his account is not about places and things or animals and plants but about people.

Even though Polo does not seem to have spoken Chinese and, as an official of the Mongol government, probably had little to do with the Chinese socially, he was eager to learn about their customs and behavior. These he recorded in an almost scientific manner with few negative comments. Unlike European missionaries who wrote about Asia, Polo was able to report different religious rites, marriage and funeral customs, and eating habits without passing judgment on the people who practiced them.

He explained, for example, that the population of China was far greater than that of Europe because men there took "six, eight, or ten wives apiece, as many as they can afford to keep, and beget innumerable children." Many men, he noted without seeming shocked, had more than thirty sons. To Polo the Buddhist Chinese were idolaters (worshippers of idols, non-Christians), but he admired their courteous manners, their interest in learning, and their profound respect for their parents.

Polo was surprised that the Chinese bathed so often—"at least three times a week" and "in winter every day." To Europeans such frequent bathing, especially in winter, was a luxury that only rich people could afford. Even more surprising, the Chinese heated the water with "a sort of black stone, which is dug out of veins in hillsides and burns like logs." Not having traveled in northern Europe where coal was already a common fuel, Polo did not recognize the black stone. He observed that the Chinese made wine from "rice and an assortment of excellent spices," which, he said, "is better to drink than any other wine."

Polo noticed the large role astrology played in Chinese lives. Even more often than Europeans of Polo's time, the Chinese consulted astrologers before making important decisions or starting a business or a voyage. Polo explained some of the differences between European and Chinese

*This Chinese celestial sphere of the astrological calendar dates from perhaps the eighth or ninth century.*

astrology, such as the twelve-year cycles of the Chinese calendar. The great khan, he said, supported five thousand astrologers in Khanbalik.

In distant regions of Kublai's empire, Polo came upon several non-Chinese ethnic groups. In the southwestern provinces, he wrote about men who covered their teeth with gold and decorated their arms and legs with tattoos. After their wives gave birth, these men went to bed, taking the baby with them, and stayed there for forty days while their wives did all the work. He wrote about people who ate raw meat and about shamans who used magic rituals to cure the sick. He remarked on sexual customs. In Tibet, parents encouraged their children to have premarital sex, and in Yunnan, husbands offered their wives to travelers passing through. In Fujian he met people who ate human flesh.

The remarkable objectivity of Polo's descriptions gave medieval Europe its first unbiased, realistic glimpse into the variety of human society in eastern Asia. Instead of the fabulous, exotic, mysterious, and imaginary East of much of European medieval literature, Polo presented real people. Instead of monsters, here were human beings.

# CHAPTER FIVE
# MARCO POLO'S BOOK

I believe it was God's will that we should return, so that
men might know the things that are in the world, since,
as we have said in the first chapter of this book, there
was never man yet, Christian or Saracen, Tartar or Pagan,
who explored so much of the world as Messer Marco,
son of Messer Niccolò Polo, great and noble citizen of
the city of Venice. THANKS BE TO GOD AMEN AMEN

—*Marco Polo, The Travels, 1299*

According to the prologue of Marco's book, the Polos had
frequently asked Kublai Khan for permission to depart, "but
he was so fond of them and so much enjoyed their company
that nothing would induce him to give them leave." Leaving
without the khan's help was out of the question: travelers
without the golden tablet of command faced arrest by the
authorities if not attack by bandits.

Fortunately for the Polos, an embassy arrived in

Khanbalik from Kublai's great nephew Arghun, the ilkhan of Persia, whose wife Queen Bulagan had recently died. In her will, the queen had requested "that no lady should sit on her throne or be wife to Arghun who was not of her lineage." The three envoys had come to China to find a new wife for Arghun from Bulagan's family.

Kublai arranged for a seventeen-year-old princess named Kokachin, who was related to Bulagan, to become Arghun's new queen. Warfare in central Asia, however, blocked overland travel back to Arghun's capital at Tabriz. It was about this time that Marco Polo returned from his sea voyage to India. He so impressed the envoys that they begged Kublai to let the Polos escort them and the princess by sea from Zaiton around Indochina and India to the port of Hormuz on the Persian Gulf. The khan "with some

*The Polos take leave of Kublai Khan in 1292. This painting is from a fifteenth-century French manuscript that included Marco Polo's book in a collection of other travel narratives.*

reluctance" agreed to let the three Polos go.

The Polos escorted Princess Kokachin and a large party of six hundred people, not counting the seamen who manned the fleet of fourteen four-masted ships. The journey proved arduous. Getting to Hormuz, the prologue reports, took about two years and cost the lives of all but eighteen of the passengers. The book reveals little about what caused such delays (other than five months spent in Sumatra, Indonesia, waiting for the monsoon winds) and so much loss of life.

## JOURNEY TO INDIA

Unlike his eyewitness accounts of Cathay and Manzi, Polo wrote about places in the Pacific and Indian oceans that he did not himself visit on his earlier sea voyage or on his journey with the Mongol princess. As a result, the chapters on southeastern and southern Asia focus more often on marvels and fabulous wealth.

The most exaggerated was Polo's account of Japan, which Polo called Cipangu. "They have gold in great abundance because it is found there in measureless quantities," he wrote. The ruler has "a very large palace entirely roofed with fine gold. . . . The value of it is almost beyond computation." Inside the palace, the floors are slabs of gold two fingers thick, and the halls and windows "are likewise adorned with gold." The fabulous wealth of Japan was probably not Polo's invention but based on false rumors Kublai spread to recruit troops to conquer the islands.

Polo offered other misleading geographical information concerning islands off the coast of China. He located Japan

1,500 miles (2,500 km) east of Cathay, when in fact it is only about 500 miles (830 km), one-third that distance. He further claimed that 7,448 islands dot the China Sea and that all produce large quantities of spices and gold. Some are so far away, he said, that Chinese ships take a year to make the round trip. He also wrote that a gulf northeast of China extended so far that it would take two months to traverse. Within it were "innumerable islands" with "quantities of gold dust."

He was similarly inaccurate about islands south of China. Depending on "the testimony of good seamen who know it well," Polo stated incorrectly that Java is the biggest island in the world and produces "all the precious spices that can be found in the world." Had he visited, he would have noticed that Java is a third the size of Sumatra (where he did land) and that although the Javanese probably traded in spices, they did not grow them.

Another island group he never visited was the Andaman Islands, possibly because the seas around them were "so turbulent and so deep that ships cannot anchor there." But, he asserted, "You may take it for a fact that all the men of this island have heads like dogs and teeth and eyes like dogs; for I assure you that the whole aspect of their faces is that of big mastiffs." Although Polo stopped short of saying that these men actually had the heads of dogs, European readers apparently imagined them that way, as the illustrations in some manuscripts of Polo's book show.

Dog traits come up again in Polo's account of Sumatra, where he said there were men with tails "fully a palm in

An early fifteenth-century French manuscript of Marco Polo's travels illustrates Polo's description of dog-headed men in the Andaman Islands.

length"—a palm equaled 9.5 or 10 inches (24 or 25 centimeters)—and "as thick as a dog's."

He reported other fictions, such as rocs, giant birds on the island of Madagascar that can pick up elephants and drop them on rocks, as gulls do clams, to smash them for food. This, he admitted, was a "second-hand account."

Nor did Polo actually witness, although he did not say so, the mining of diamonds in southeastern India. According to his account, the diamonds lie at the bottom of deep gorges infested with poisonous snakes. To get the diamonds, men threw raw meat into the gorges, the meat attracted eagles, and the eagles flew off with the diamond-encrusted meat. All the men had to do was surprise the eagles as they ate, scare them off, and pluck diamonds from the remaining meat. The men then mined more diamonds from the eagles' droppings.

# A HANDBOOK OF SOUTH ASIA: PEARLS, PARROTS, AND PEOPLE

These examples of misinformation are the exception. For the most part, Polo was eager to correct many errors found in earlier accounts of the East. He was concerned to prove that the European pictures of unicorns were wrong, for he saw one-horned animals in Sumatra, "scarcely smaller than elephants" that "spend their time by preference wallowing in mud and slime" and "are very ugly brutes to look at." These "unicorns" were obviously rhinoceroses.

Polo was convinced that the griffin, a mythical beast said to be half lion and half eagle, was really the roc. He had heard that this giant bird lived on Madagascar, although he apparently did not realize it too was a mythical creature. People who claimed to have seen pygmies, he pointed out, had really only seen shrunken dried monkeys made to look like small humans.

The chapters on Indochina, India, and nearby islands continue to show Polo's scientific interest in plants, animals, products, and people. In Sumatra he gathered seeds for brazilwood, a tropical tree used for dyeing and in cabinetry. That the seeds failed to grow in Venice was, he concluded, "due to the cold climate." He explained how southern Asians made sago flour and palm wine from palm trees, dived for pearls, and harpooned whales.

For every region, he supplied information about crops—camphor, brazilwood, pepper, ginger, indigo, cotton—and reported on birds and beasts—parrots "as white as snow," peacocks "much bigger and handsomer" than European ones, "black lions" (panthers), "Maimon cats" (baboons),

A fourteenth-century French illustration from a manuscript of Marco Polo's book shows people of Sumatra gathering sap from palm trees to make wine.

and along the east coast of Africa (considered part of Asia in Polo's time), lions and giraffes.

As elsewhere, Polo showed a merchant's appreciation of gemstones—especially the sapphires, topazes, amethysts, garnets, and "superb and authentic rubies" of Sri Lanka—and a lively interest in trade. Northwestern India, he observed, imported brass and horses, while exporting cotton cloth and leather goods.

Throughout, Polo's curiosity about human customs in southeastern and southern Asia is on display. He mentions clothing (very little of which was worn in the tropical climate), funeral rites (and the custom of widows being cremated with the bodies of their husbands), superstitions (such as avoiding business during unlucky hours of the day), habits (such as chewing the leaf of the betel palm), and religious practices. He retells the story of Buddha and shows great admiration for his virtuous life. "Had he been a Christian," Polo asserts, "he would have been a great saint with our Lord Jesus Christ."

Polo's enthusiasm for India is as great if not greater than his praise for China. "Greater India" (probably modern India, Pakistan, and Bangladesh) is "the richest and most splendid province in the world."

## THE LAST LEG OF THE JOURNEY

When the Polos reached Arghun's land, they discovered that the ilkhan had died. Arghun's son Ghazan, however, was happy to take the princess as his wife. The prologue reports that the princess wept to see them go, for she had become "deeply attached to the three men." The four had, after all, spent two years together on a difficult voyage that had claimed the lives of most of their fellow passengers.

After a lengthy stay in Tabriz, the Polos resumed their journey. There was no question of going back to China. Kublai Khan had died in 1294. Possibly, the Polos heard the news while they were in Tabriz. Besides, the elder Polos were no doubt eager to see their homeland. With horses, provisions, and guides supplied by their golden tablets of command, the Polos trekked overland from Tabriz northwest to the Black Sea.

As they passed through Trebizond (a Greek kingdom on the southeastern shore of the Black Sea) to embark on a ship to Constantinople, the authorities seized part of the

The Polos arrive at Hormuz at the end of their sea trip from China. This illustration is from a fifteenth-century French manuscript.

goods the Polos had brought with them from China. We know about this setback, which is not mentioned in Polo's book, only because the Grand Council of Venice later sued the ruler of Trebizond for the return of the Polos' goods. They were worth four thousand Byzantine *hyperpyra*—a large sum of money equal to one thousand pounds of raw silk. When Maffeo Polo wrote his will in 1310, he was still waiting for the money to be repaid.

## A DRAMATIC ARRIVAL IN VENICE

Several colorful stories exist about the Polos' return home sometime in 1295. None of the stories were written down in Polo's lifetime or even soon afterward. Only in the 1550s did the scholar Giovanni Battista Ramusio, also a

Venetian, write the first account of the Polos' return. He based his story on what he had heard as a child from an old man who lived near the Polo family home and who had heard it from his father and grandfather. Even assuming that these men fathered their children at unusually old ages, this chain of storytellers does not reach back to 1295. Nor is it likely that the story remained the same over two and a half centuries.

The Polos, Ramusio writes, looked very different after twenty-four years in Asia. "They were quite changed in aspect, and had got a certain indescribable smack of the Tartar both in air and accent, having indeed all but forgotten their Venetian tongue. Their clothes too were coarse and shabby, and of a Tartar cut." As a result, when they reached the Polo palazzo (which Ramusio did not know was most likely purchased after the Polos' return), their relatives "flatly refused to believe" that they were Nicolo, Maffeo, and Marco Polo.

To convince the family of their identity, Ramusio's story continues, the Polos invited all their relatives to a grand feast. They wore elegant clothes of satin, damask, and velvet, changing them as the dinner progressed and cutting up the clothes they took off to give to the servants. At the end of the meal, Marco Polo brought out the coarse, shabby clothes they had worn on their arrival. He took a sharp knife and stabbed the seams. "Jewels of the greatest value" poured forth "in vast quantities." These "rubies, sapphires, carbuncles [possibly garnets], diamonds, and emeralds" had been stitched into their outfits to hide them from thieves and pirates on their journey home.

The amazed family now welcomed them with open arms, Ramusio concludes. All Venice "flocked to the house to embrace them."

## SIR MARCO MILLIONS

Polo's fame spread quickly. In Venice his stories—and possibly also those told by his father and uncle—attracted attention even before the book was written. Ramusio says that Polo used the word *millions* so often when speaking of the great khan's wealth that Venetians gave him the nickname Sir Marco Millions. Soon all three Polos were called Millions.

A contemporary writer, however, asserts that the name *Millions* came from the treasures the Polos brought back from Asia. Calling the Polos Millions, he says, was like calling them millionaires. The Polos were indeed well off, for they bought a large palazzo with a tower. (Only its two small courtyards— suitably named Corti del

This eighteenth-century water-color by a German artist depicts Marco Polo in Mongol dress. According to legend, the Polos weren't recognized when they arrived in Venice partly because of their Mongol clothing.

Milione, "Courtyards of the Millions"—remain.) They lived comfortable lives, yet they were not especially wealthy. The possessions listed in their wills were not unusual for the Venetian noble class. Whatever the original reason for the name, it stuck so well that in modern Italy, Polo's book carries the title *Il Milione (The Millions)*.

## TO PRISON IN GENOA

Hostilities between Venice and Genoa grew worse while the Polos were away. Since the prologue to Marco Polo's book says that Polo wrote the book while in a Genoese prison, it is generally agreed that his capture took place during that conflict.

The rivalry between Genoa and Venice was an all-out war. Battles were not limited to naval engagements. Warships from both sides attacked one another's merchant convoys. On land, merchants set fire to one another's trading colonies. Some historians believe that Marco Polo took up trading after his return to Venice and was traveling on a merchant ship when the Genoese captured him and imprisoned him in Genoa.

Ramusio, however, tells a different story. In 1298 Venice sent ninety galleys to challenge the Genoese fleet near the island of Korcula in the Adriatic Sea off the coast of Croatia. Ramusio says that Marco Polo was put in command of one of the galleys. In the battle, Polo "pressed on in the vanguard of the attack" and fought "with high and worthy courage in the defense of his country and his kindred," but not receiving "due support" from the other ships and being

According to one story, Marco Polo was in command of one of the Venetian ships during the battle near Korcula. This woodcut shows him standing on the ship's deck.

wounded, he was taken and "immediately put in irons and sent to Genoa."

The battle near Korcula was the largest engagement of the long war between the two cities. Both sides suffered heavy losses. One source says that only twelve Venetian ships escaped. The rest were sunk, captured, or burned by the Genoese. Several thousand Venetians were taken prisoner, among them the Venetian commander, who committed suicide to avoid the humiliation of being paraded in Genoa.

Did Marco Polo command a galley in this battle? Or did his name become associated with it simply because it was the most memorable encounter of the war? No one can say for sure.

## WRITING IN PRISON

The prologue relates that while in prison, Polo, "to occupy his leisure as well as to afford entertainment to readers," had a

## ETCHED IN STONE

One of the primary sources of information about the Battle of Korcula is found on the walls of the Church of Saint Matthew in Genoa. During the Middle Ages, Saint Matthew's was the private church of the Doria family. The victorious commander of the Genoese fleet, Lamba Doria, is buried there. Details of his victory are inscribed on the marble facade of the church.

fellow prisoner, Rustichello of Pisa, write down "all the things he had seen and had heard by true report." The prison was evidently no dank dungeon but a place with writing materials and perhaps even some comfort. Two contemporary accounts draw very different pictures of how the Genoese treated their many prisoners: one says they were treated kindly; another says that most of the prisoners died of hunger.

Ramusio's account adds a few details to what is in the prologue, but not all are helpful. Polo's stories attracted so much attention, Ramusio wrote, that Genoese noblemen came to visit him every day. Polo became more of a celebrity than a prisoner. Tired of repeating his stories, Polo followed someone's suggestion to write them down. He sent a letter to his father in Venice asking him for the notes he had kept during his travels. One of the Genoese gentlemen assisted him by writing the book in Latin. We know from the book, however, that Rustichello was from Pisa not Genoa and the surviving manu-scripts suggest that the book was first written in Franco-Italian, the Italian-accented French spoken in Italy, and not in Latin.

Even so, many scholars think Ramusio may have been right about the notes because it is hard to imagine that Polo worked entirely from memory. Some historians, however, argue that medieval people had better memories than people do today and were less dependent on writing things down. They think that Polo dictated most, if not all, of the book from memory. That might account for some of the book's inconsistencies, errors, and exaggerated numbers.

No one knows exactly how Polo and Rustichello worked together on the

This Volume Two title page from the Henry Yule 1874 edition of Marco Polo's book shows Marco Polo in prison dictating his story to Rustichello.

book. Polo had all the information, but Rustichello was an experienced writer. Polo may have dictated the book to Rustichello, or he may have told him about his travels and let Rustichello compose the actual sentences and scenes, much the way modern ghostwriters help people who are not professional writers set down their memoirs. Most likely, it was some combination of the two.

The prologue to the book, for example, seems to be Rustichello's summary. "Our book," he promises readers, tells of "all the great wonders and curiosities" of Asia, "as they were related by Messer Marco Polo." In the book itself, however, Polo sometimes speaks in the first person. One passage begins: "When I, Marco, was at the court of the Great Khan . . ." Thus it seems that some parts were dictated and written down in Polo's words and other parts summarized or retold by Rustichello. Phrasing that resembles Rustichello's writing in another work is most evident in the prologue and in the history of Mongol wars at the end of the book.

Genoa and Venice signed a peace treaty in the summer of 1299, and the prisoners were released. If Polo were captured at the battle near Korcula, which took place September 8, 1298, Polo and Rustichello had less than a year to complete the book. It seems likely that either Polo was captured earlier or the two men continued to work together after they were freed—or both. At least one event in the book suggests that Polo added information after leaving prison. A Mongol battle described toward the end of the book took place in 1299. Polo probably heard about the battle only after he returned to Venice.

## THE TRAVELS OF POLO'S BOOK

Once the book was complete, possibly even before, Polo would have made his work public by reading it to his family and friends. He may also have had copies made to present to important Venetian citizens. A fifteenth-century manuscript reports that a copy of the book was kept chained near the Rialto for merchants to consult. Venetians were soon reading and talking about Marco Polo's book. Before long, handwritten copies made their way to other towns in northern Italy and across the Alps to France.

In 1310 Pietro d'Abano, a professor of philosophy and natural science at the University of Padua, praised Polo's discoveries. He observed that Polo's reports from tropical islands resolved the question many European geographers had as to whether lands along the equator were too hot for people to live in. He also took an interest in Polo's astronomical observations from the Southern Hemisphere. D'Abano called Marco Polo, "the most extensive traveller and the most diligent inquirer whom I have ever known."

A fourteenth-century historian from Florence, Giovanni Villani, lists *Il Milione* as a good source of information about the Mongols. He says the book was written by "Messer Marco Polo of Venice, who tells much about their power and dominion, having spent a long time among them."

Meanwhile in Bologna, Friar Francesco Pipino was busily rewriting the book in Latin. In a preface, Pipino says that his superiors in the Catholic Church asked him to translate the book. He promises the reader that the book will show them "the variety, beauty, and vastness of God's Creation" and move them "to strive for the diffusion of the Christian Faith" among non-Christian nations. He vouches for Polo as "a most respectable, veracious, and devout person" whose "many virtues claim entire belief for that which he relates."

In 1307 a French envoy asked Marco Polo for a copy of the book for Charles, Count of Valois, son of the king of France. The translation prepared for Charles was probably the first in the language of northern France. It became the source for many more copies in French. Eighteen manuscripts in this version of French survive. Other than books composed in

Latin, Polo's was the first book written by an Italian to be translated into the language of a country outside Italy.

Polo's work was well received by scholars, churchmen, and statesmen of his time, but some people had their doubts about Polo's "marvels." Jacopo d'Acqui, who devoted a short chapter of *Imago Mundi* (Picture of the World) to Marco Polo, says that Polo did not include many things in his book because he knew that people would accuse him of lying. "And because there are many great and strange things in that Book, which are reckoned past all credence, [Polo] was asked by his friends on his death-bed to correct the Book by removing everything that went beyond the facts. To which his reply was that he had not told *one-half* of what he had really seen!"

## MARCO POLO'S LATER YEARS

At some point after being freed from prison, Marco Polo, by then in his mid-forties, married Donata Badoer, who came from one of the oldest and best-known noble families of Venice. The couple had three daughters, Fantina, Bellela, and Moreta, all of whom married Venetian noblemen.

No letters, diaries, or other personal documents concerning Polo survive. To piece together how he lived his remaining days, scholars have only legal papers, such as law cases and wills. These sources show him still slightly involved in commerce—he made loans and collected a commission on the sale of some musk. But for the most part, it is his cousins, his half brother (his father had remarried between his two journeys to China), and other members of the Polo family who are mentioned in records of travel to the Greek island of Crete and to the port of Tana on the Black Sea to trade in cinnamon, pepper, incense, ginger, and sugar and to Apulia in southern Italy for grain. One cousin lost valuable cargo and perished in a terrible shipwreck.

Did Polo take sides in the dramatic revolt of June 15, 1310, when the common people rose up against the Grand Council of Venice? Did he meet the Florentine poet Dante when he visited Venice in 1322? We don't know. Court documents only speak of selling and buying property and settling debts. They are valuable sources of dates, family relationships, and financial standing. But they lack personality. Unfortunately, the sharp, curious, energetic man that the reader can detect from the *Travels* left no written account of his later years.

Two documents offer brief glimpses of Polo after his return. In 1324, on his deathbed, Polo signed his last will and testament. His bequests to the church, monasteries, hospitals, individual friars, and charitable organizations remind us of his Christian faith and suggest a generous nature. We also learn that Polo owned a slave, Peter the Tartar, whom he released from bondage in his will. In addition, he forgave Peter all his debts and left him some money, which perhaps helped him a few years later to become a naturalized citizen of Venice.

The rest of Polo's estate went to his wife and daughters, not to male relatives as often occurred. The loving father was careful to stipulate that his daughters' portions were to be equal, but only after setting aside dowry and wedding costs for his youngest, who was not yet married.

Many years later, Fantina's husband died and Fantina had

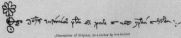

Marco Polo's will, which was written in 1324

to go to court to regain her dowry and her proper inheritance from her father, which had become part of her husband's estate. One of the documents presented as evidence in the suit is a list of her father's possessions at the time of his death. There, sandwiched among a variety of everyday household goods, a few items glimmer with hints of Polo's exciting life— several fine fabrics from China, a silver belt in Mongolian style, Buddhist prayer beads, a Mongol headdress adorned with gold and pearls (which one historian suggests had belonged to Princess Kokachin), and one of the famous gold tablets of command that guaranteed the Polos safe passage through the Mongol Empire.

# Marco Polo's Legacy

Tonight at midnight I weighed anchors from the island of Isabela . . . to go to the island of Cuba, which I heard from these people was very large and of great commerce and that there were there gold and spices and great ships and merchants. . . . And I believe . . . that it is the island of Cipango of which marvelous things are told. And in the spheres that I saw and in world maps it is in this region.

—Christopher Columbus, Diario [Diary] of his first voyage to America, Wednesday, October 24, 1492

Far more valuable than the gold tablet of command, the princess's headdress, or any treasure Polo brought back from Asia was the book he left to posterity. After Polo's death, it continued to attract readers. From the time that a German printer first set Polo's words in type more than five centuries ago, The Travels has not gone out of print. Modern readers still find Marco Polo's book a fascinating window on medieval Asia. It has inspired numerous modern novels,

poems, plays, and movies as well as travel books by
adventurous writers intent on tracing the Polos' routes from
Venice to China and back.

Aside from its educational and entertainment value,
Polo's book also had an impact on the course of history.
More than any other account written during the brief period
when Europeans traveled across the Mongol Empire to trade

The Spanish manuscript version of Marco Polo's
book is dated 1503.

and spread Christianity, Marco Polo's book taught Europeans about Asian geography, people, and resources. Europeans already knew about many useful and valuable Asian products. Polo was the first to spell out exactly where they came from and to describe, in detail, for a large, literate audience the cultures that produced them.

During the fourteenth century, merchants, missionaries, and other travelers from Europe braved the journey to central Asia, China, and India. Instead of depending on Muslim middlemen, as had earlier generations of merchants, these

# MARCO POLO: FACT OR FICTION?

Legends about Marco Polo probably began to sprout soon after he and his father and uncle returned to Venice with tales about the great khan and his fabulous empire. Giovanni Battista Ramusio's edition of Polo's book in 1559 added to the folklore with stories about the feast the Polos held to prove their identity to their relatives and Polo's heroic role in the war with Genoa. Polo became so famous that rumor began to credit him with introducing a variety of Chinese inventions to Europe, among them the magnetic compass, gunpowder, the printing press, even spaghetti (which Polo no doubt ate plenty of as a child in Venice), and ice cream (which did not reach Italy until the 1600s). Not one of these claims is true. But they are all good examples of how fame attracts even more fame.

Europeans ventured inland to trade directly with the sources of supply. A Florentine writer assured merchants that "the road leading from Tana [on the Black Sea] to Cathay is quite safe both by day and by night." But a series of events soon closed overland access to eastern Asia.

## THE SILK ROADS CLOSE

In the 1330s, somewhere on the central steppes of Asia or on the borders of India and China, the plague bacterium, *Yersinia pestis*, began to spread from wild gerbils or ground squirrels to rats in villages and towns. Fleas leaving the dead rats carried the germs to people. The result was the Black Death, an epidemic of bubonic plague. From ports in western Asia, ships transported the fatal bacteria to North Africa and Europe. By 1353 between one-third and one-half of the population of Europe, North Africa, and many parts of Asia had died.

The outbreak of bubonic plague in the mid-fourteenth century was one of the greatest catastrophes in human history. With the enormous loss of population came widespread economic depression. Production and trade dwindled across Asia and Europe.

Political changes in the Mongol Empire between the mid-1300s and the mid-1400s also disrupted trade. The khans of the Golden Horde converted to Islam and became less tolerant of Christian merchants and missionaries. Turkish rebels captured Constantinople in 1453 and established the Muslim Ottoman Empire. Another Turkish leader, Timur the Lame, or Tamerlane, overran modern-day Afghanistan, Iran, Iraq, northern India, Syria, and Turkey in

E nfuere alerent chafcu roz
az ether loz euer a befoing
az out loz coment aqcrc loing
2 i fulz le roi furent ploze
2 uoz qil furent enterre

S arqeus ozaur tro
S iles mufhet enz a
d eles laur fiure b
E ntrare furent r

A la pline belle ten

An outbreak of bubonic plague ravaged Asia, Europe, and North Africa in the 1340s. This illustration is from a fourteenth-century Italian manuscript.

a forty-year career of ruthless conquest.

Meanwhile, in eastern Asia, Chinese peasants overthrew the last Mongol emperor in 1368 and established the Ming dynasty. During the fifteenth century, Ming emperors withdrew from overland and overseas trade.

Thus, one by one, the links in the chain that had made the Polos' journey possible broke apart. All the caravan routes across Asia that nineteenth-century writers called the Silk Roads closed to Christian traders from Europe.

## SEEKING NEW TRADE ROUTES FOR ASIAN GOODS

Venice continued to trade with Egypt, but once again, Muslim nations controlled both land and sea trade in Asia.

They charged high duties on goods traveling to Europe. The cost of spices and other Asian products—Chinese silks and porcelain, Persian carpets and tapestries, and gemstones from Sri Lanka—rose steeply.

Spices were not just a matter of flavorings. Spices, especially pepper, were essential for food preservation in an age with no refrigeration. Spices was also an umbrella-term for a variety of goods that included medicines, perfumes, dyes, and other industrial products such as alum (aluminum sulfate), which was used in dyeing cloth, tanning leather, and making glass. Spices were crucial to Europe's economic growth.

Merchants across Europe looked eagerly for new trade routes. From every seaboard country, ships ventured out in search of ocean routes to Asia—whether by attempting to sail south around Africa, north through the Arctic Ocean, or west across the Atlantic. For these explorers, Marco Polo's book supplied the best geographical information about Asia available in Europe.

Polo's work had already influenced mapmakers, who during the fifteenth century began to correct older ideas about Asia. Using information from Polo's book, they added places such as Cathay, Manzi, Kinsai, Zaiton, Khanbalik, and Cipangu to their charts. One of these up-to-date maps was prepared for King Afonso V of Portugal around 1457.

As printed books began to replace handwritten manuscripts in the second half of the fifteenth century, several printers published copies of Marco Polo's book. It was certain to sell well. More Europeans were learning to read, and all Europe was eager to know more about eastern Asia. Among the men who consulted Marco Polo's book were

Prince Henry of Portugal, called the Navigator, and an explorer named Christopher Columbus from Genoa. Columbus's well-thumbed copy of Polo's book is in a library in Seville, Spain. Columbus's handwritten comments mark the margins of the book.

## POLO'S TRAVELS AND COLUMBUS'S DISCOVERY OF AMERICA

Columbus may not have read Marco Polo's book before his first voyage west, but he was well aware of information in it. Columbus's captains, an eyewitness reported, recruited sailors in 1492 by telling them they were going to a land with "houses roofed with gold." The words clearly echo (and exaggerate) Polo's description of the royal palace in Cipangu.

But it wasn't just Polo's report of "measureless quantities" of gold in Japan that lured Columbus across the Atlantic Ocean. Other erroneous information in Polo's book—that Japan was 1,500 miles (2,400 km) east of mainland Asia and that 7,448 islands rich in gold and spices dotted the China Sea, some of them several months' journey east of Zaiton—also played a role. Columbus knew about these islands because, as he mentions in the logbook of his first voyage, he had seen them on globes and maps.

In planning his voyage, Columbus had to figure out how far away from western Europe all these reported islands were. That depended on how large the world actually was. In the 1470s, Paolo dal Pozzo Toscanelli, a physician and astrologer from Florence with a great interest in maps, calculated that only 5,000 nautical miles (9,000 km) separated Cathay from the Canary Islands in the Atlantic Ocean off the coast of northwestern Africa. He sent this information in a letter to an adviser to the Portuguese king Afonso V, together with many details about Kinsai and Cipangu from Polo's book. Some historians think that Columbus saw this letter.

Columbus chiseled down the distances even more. By underestimating the number of miles in a degree of longitude as well as the number of degrees between China and Europe, Columbus believed he had only 2,400 miles (3,800 km) to sail between the Canary Islands and Japan.

Thus Polo's exaggerations and Columbus's miscalculations led to the expedition that landed in the West Indies in 1492. Sailors from northern Europe had reached North America before Columbus, but the Spanish-financed discovery was the first organized by a major monarchy intent on expansion and conquest. It changed the course of world history.

## HERO TO THE AGE OF EXPLORATION AND EUROPEAN EXPANSION

Others besides Columbus felt the power of Polo's words. An age of exploration had begun. In 1488, while Columbus sought financial backing for his westward voyage, Portuguese ships led by Bartolomeu Dias that were trying to reach the East by sailing around Africa reached the southern tip of that continent. While Spanish ships explored the Americas (still thinking it was part of Asia), the Portuguese navigator Vasco da Gama sailed into the Indian Ocean and landed on the Malabar Coast of India. England, not to be left out, sent

John Cabot to North America to explore the coast of Newfoundland, where English and Irish ships had found rich fishing grounds. Soon ships from France, Holland, Denmark, Sweden, and Russia joined the explorations.

Even though Polo's geographical information was being revised and supplemented by European explorers, his popularity did not wane. During the sixteenth century, twenty-four new editions of Marco Polo's book appeared, sometimes printed together with other accounts by travelers to distant places. New translations appeared in Portuguese, Spanish, French, Italian, German, English, and Latin, which was still an international language used by European scholars and diplomats.

Before long, mapmakers who at first had added China to the Cathay and Manzi of Marco Polo's book realized that all three were names for the same country. They corrected their maps accordingly. As Europeans rediscovered Asia, Polo's place-names (usually in Persian or Mongol, not Chinese) disappeared from maps.

But Polo's name did not disappear. Instead, he became a hero to the age, extolled as the first and greatest of explorers. An English writer in 1549 finds him "more illustrious and worthy of praise [than Columbus and other later explorers] for having opened the world to the following generations." Ironically, it was mainly Polo's misinformation, based on hearsay, and his tendency to exaggerate that awoke in Europeans a restless desire to see for themselves the distant realms he described, as well as to gain access to the many resources he listed.

Polo's fame also grew in part because more and more people recognized what he had accomplished in crossing Asia and gathering so much information. His book is a valuable firsthand source of information about the Mongol Empire and the Yuan dynasty in China. Historians note that Polo provides "the most complete and trustworthy description" of the Mongol military organization, praise his objectivity in a time when religious tolerance was rare among Europeans, and find his book "an inexhaustible mine of information" about everyday customs of Asian peoples in the thirteenth century, "always reliable and valuable as a starting point for further research on the Asia of his times."

Fame has made Polo larger than life. His name has become a symbol of travel, adventure, exploration, and learning. The airport in Venice is named for him. Travel agencies, ships, streets, bridges, a satellite, and a steam engine carry his name. There is a Marco Polo Cycling Club and a Marco Polo website that provides Internet content for classrooms. Satellites, steam engines, bicycles, and computers are all inventions Polo would have loved to see. In many ways, his book helped make them possible, for it ushered in a new "going-there-to-find-out" way of thinking. As scientists debate sending an astronaut to Mars, we can see that Polo's legacy lives on.

# DID MARCO POLO GO TO CHINA?

Some historians question whether Marco Polo really went to China. If he did, they ask, why didn't he mention the Great Wall? Or other Chinese customs, such as binding the feet of upper-class women, drinking tea, fishing with trained cormorants, or writing with brushes? Why didn't he notice that the Chinese had printed books? Why is there no record of his name in Chinese histories of the time? And why are all the place-names in the Persian or Mongol language?

Polo's book, however, is so full of accurate descriptions of people, places, and customs in Mongol China that it seems much more likely the Polos were there than that they were somewhere else during their twenty-four years away from Venice. Polo scholars offer a variety of responses:

• The Great Wall was in disrepair in the thirteenth century. Other European visitors after Polo's time do not mention it either. The wall that modern tourists visit was built in the sixteenth century.

• Upper-class Chinese women did not generally go out in public. Polo did not speak Chinese and probably did not mix socially with upper-class Chinese families.

• Mongols and northern Chinese did not usually drink tea. It was primarily a custom in southern China, where Polo seems to have spent less time.

- Polo was a civil servant for the Mongol government and lived among Mongols and other foreigners. He tended to overlook Kublai Khan's Chinese subjects.

- Persian and Mongol were the principal languages used in the Mongol Empire. Maps and official documents used Mongol or Persian spellings for Chinese place-names. Polo may have brought such a map or documents back with him from China.

- Since Polo did not know Chinese, he may not have noticed their writing or their books.

- Although Polo does say (although not in all the manuscripts) that he was governor of Yangzhou, it is more likely that the role he played was not so great as to be mentioned in contemporary Chinese sources.

- Given the differences among the manuscripts, in which some have information not included in others, it is possible that some omissions were simply bits of information lost during the copying process.

- Perhaps the story told of Polo on his deathbed is true: he did not tell half of what he saw!

# PRIMARY SOURCE RESEARCH

To learn about historical events, people study many sources, such as books, websites, newspaper articles, photographs, and paintings. These sources can be separated into two general categories—primary sources and secondary sources.

A primary source is the record of an eyewitness. Primary sources provide firsthand accounts about a person or event. Examples include diaries, letters, autobiographies, speeches, newspapers, and oral history interviews. Libraries, archives, historical societies, and museums often have primary sources available on-site or on the Internet.

A secondary source is published information that was researched, collected, and written or otherwise created by someone who was not an eyewitness. These authors or artists use primary sources and other secondary sources in their research, but they interpret and arrange the source material in their own works. Secondary sources include history books, novels, biographies, movies, documentaries, and magazines. Libraries and museums are filled with secondary sources.

After finding primary and secondary sources, authors and historians must evaluate them. They may ask questions such as: Who created this document? What is this person's point of view? What biases might this person have? How trustworthy is this document? Just because a person was an eyewitness to an event does not mean that person recorded the whole truth about that event. For example, a soldier describing a battle might depict only the heroic actions of his unit and only the brutal behavior of the enemy. An account from a soldier on the opposing side might portray the same battle very differently. When sources disagree, researchers must decide through additional study which explanation makes the most sense. For this reason, historians consult a variety of primary and secondary sources. Then they can draw their own conclusions.

The Pivotal Moments in History series takes readers on a journey to important junctures in history that shaped our modern world. Authors researched each event using both primary and secondary sources, an approach that enhances readers' awareness of the complexities of the materials and helps bring to life the rich stories from which we draw our understanding of our shared history.

## LEARNING ABOUT MARCO POLO

Almost everything we know about Marco Polo comes from the book that he and his fellow prisoner of war, Rustichello of Pisa, wrote in prison in Genoa, Italy, around 1298–1299. Since the printing press did not yet exist in Europe, each copy of Polo's book had to be made by someone writing with a quill pen and ink on parchment (made from sheepskin), vellum (made from calfskin), or paper.

Polo's book was much in demand as soon as it was written. One by one, hundreds of copies were made. Of these, one hundred and fifty manuscripts and fragments of manuscripts survive today. Polo's original manuscript, however, is not among them.

# PUBLICATION IN MANUSCRIPT

As with most manuscripts of a medieval work, each handwritten copy of Polo's book differs from the others in small or large ways. A person copying a manuscript may make simple mistakes, like skipping a paragraph as his eye moves back and forth between the original and his copy. He may misread the handwriting on the manuscript he is copying, misspell unfamiliar place-names, or misunderstand a passage.

A copyist may also decide to make changes to a book. Perhaps he wants to comment about what he is reading or tell a story that it reminds him of. He might choose to cut out passages that he considers too boring, too shocking, or too incredible.

For almost two hundred years, handwritten copies of Marco Polo's book passed from reader to reader. Wealthy men and women hired scribes to copy the book on fine parchment, artists to illustrate the work, and bookbinders to produce splendid leather-bound volumes decorated with gold. The Duchess of Burgundy (Burgundy is part of modern France) ordered a copy in 1312. King Charles V of France, who reigned from 1364 to 1380, had five copies in the royal library.

# THE LANGUAGES OF POLO'S BOOK

Scholars of Polo's work believe that Polo and Rusticello wrote the original manuscript (which no longer exists) in French. If so, it was a good choice in a book they hoped would attract many readers. In the late 1200s, educated Europeans learned several languages. At home and in the marketplace, people

Manuscript illuminators in medieval Europe used European features and dress for Asian subjects. This illustration from a manuscript in the British Library in London shows Kublai Khan feasting at his court.

used local dialects. Venetian, Genoese, and Tuscan were spoken in Venice, Genoa, and Tuscany (a region in northwestern Italy that includes the cities of Florence and Pisa). Latin was the language used in church, law courts, and books of philosophy and science. French was considered the best language for works of literature, for French was the language of polite society, spoken by both women and men of the upper classes. Like Latin, French crossed borders. From Scotland to Bohemia (today's Czech Republic) and from

Sweden to Italy, the aristocracy knew French.

French was so widespread that it varied from place to place. Marco Polo and Rustichello most likely spoke French with an Italian accent and a little Italian mixed in. Some scholars call this language Franco-Italian. The earliest surviving manuscript of Polo's book is in that language. When Marco Polo had a copy of his book made for a member of the French royal family in 1307, scribes "corrected" the language to suit northern French ears—much as today's publishers in the United States may adapt the English in books from Great Britain for U.S. audiences.

In some countries, the work was translated into other languages and dialects. Within twenty years, the book was circulating in German, Venetian, Tuscan, and even Latin versions. Not many medieval manuscripts were translated into Latin. That a Dominican friar (a member of a Christian religious order founded by St. Dominic in 1216) was commissioned to write a Latin translation of the book illustrates how important the Roman Catholic Church considered the information Polo provided about Asia to be.

As the book traveled farther from Venice, other translations appeared. Manuscripts survive that were written in Irish Gaelic, Aragonese (a dialect of Spanish), and Czech.

## FROM SCRIPT TO PRINT

In the late fifteenth century, Europeans began reproducing books on printing presses. The first printed copy of Polo's book appeared in Nuremberg, Germany, in 1477. By the end of the sixteenth century, twenty-six more printed editions were published in many languages. The book's popularity continues. In the 1980s, one scholar counted 280 printed editions of Polo's work. The printed editions of Marco Polo's book also vary greatly since they are based on different manuscripts. Some editors followed one manuscript or a group of similar manuscripts. Others put very different manuscripts together like pieces of a great puzzle.

Modern editors make thousands of decisions as they try to produce a book that they believe is as close as possible to the original manuscript that Polo and Rustichello wrote. Sometimes teams of editors work together because the task of combing through the many manuscripts and editions is so demanding. No amount of scholarship, however, can reconstruct the original manuscript. For this reason, the Polo books available today are technically not primary sources.

Readers of English have many versions to choose from. There are early translations written in the English of Shakespeare's time, several translations from the nineteenth century, often with pages of notes to help the reader, and many modern renditions. The finest and most scholarly translation in English is the one by Arthur C. Moule and Paul Pelliot, which attempts "to weave together all, or nearly all, the extant [existing] words which have ever claimed to be Marco Polo."

Anyone writing about Marco Polo faces a difficult choice. Which of the many versions of *The Travels* (as Polo's book is usually called in English) is the best to use as a source? For this book, the author chose to use the Ronald Latham translation, first published in 1958.

# WHAT WAS THAT BOOK CALLED?

Medieval manuscripts were generally more casual about titles than are modern books. Scribes often copied a variety of works and bound them together. Parchment and paper were too expensive for separate title pages. Instead, the scribe generally indicated the end of one work with an "explicit," which is an abbreviation of the Latin phrase *explicitus est liber,* meaning "the book is ended." The Latin term *incipit* often marked the beginning of the next work. Brief descriptions inserted after an explicit or an incipit served as titles.

Here are some titles found in Polo manuscripts:

*Explicit Liber Milionis:* Here ends the Book of Millions

*Explicit le Livre nomme du Grant Caan de la Graunt Cite de Cambaluc:* Here ends the book called The Great Khan of the Great City of Khanbalik

It has many advantages. It is based on the edition edited by Professor Luigi Foscolo Benedetto, first published in Italy in 1928, that is most widely accepted and used by Polo scholars. It is also written in clear, readable prose. The language is modern, yet it keeps enough of Rustichello's medieval style to suggest the flavor of the earliest manuscripts. Finally, it is easily available in bookstores and libraries today.

*Cy après commence le liure de Marc Paule des merveilles daise la grant et dinde la majour et mineur*: Below this begins Marco Polo's book about the Marvels of Greater Asia and Greater and Lesser India

*Ce Livre est des Merveilles du Monde*: This book is about the Marvels of the World

*Ci commence . . . le Devisement du Monde*: Here begins the Description of the World

Early printed versions of the book were equally inconsistent. Pipino's Latin version was titled *De condicionibus et consuetudinibus orientalium regionum*, meaning "Concerning the Conditions and Customs of Eastern Regions." In the 1550s, Ramusio first came up with the catchy title used in most current English editions: *The Travels of Marco Polo*.

# FINDING OUT MORE ABOUT MARCO POLO

To learn other information about Marco Polo and his times, scholars turn to various primary sources. About seventy-five legal documents survive concerning Marco Polo, members of his family, and their descendants. Marco Polo, his uncles, his half brother, and two cousins wrote wills that provide details of family life, such as where they lived and what they owned. The family is also mentioned in other official documents concerning lawsuits, export licenses, loans, and sales of property. Some of these Latin documents have been translated into modern Italian and a few into English.

The history of Venice written by Martino da Canale in the 1270s gives information about what was happening in Venice during Polo's boyhood. Da Canale, like Polo later, wrote in French, and his chronicle is available in modern Italian, but not in English. Another man named Da Canal (without the final e) signed his name in a notebook full of math problems and other information that was probably compiled by a student in the early 1300s. Known as the *Zibaldone da Canal* (Da Canal's Notebook), this collection of writings shows what a young nobleman, like Polo, needed to know to transact business in Venice. An English translation was published in 1994.

Other travel accounts by Europeans in Asia before and after Polo went there add to our knowledge of the people and places he wrote about. Several friars wrote about their travels to Mongolia and China to spread Christianity. Mongol and Chinese histories also help fill out a picture of Marco Polo's world. Rashid al-Din Tabib's history of the Mongol rulers in the mid to late 1200s and Chau Ju-kua's account of Chinese and Arab trade in the twelfth and thirteenth centuries, for example, offer glimpses of daily life in central and eastern Asia. Many of these sources have been published in English translation.

# MEDIEVAL BEST SELLERS

The number of surviving manuscripts of a work provides a rough gauge of how popular it was. In modern times, books sell thousands or even millions of copies, but before the printing press, far fewer copies were made. Here are some popular medieval works and the number of their surviving manuscripts:

| | |
|---|---|
| Geoffrey of Monmouth's *History of the Kings of Britain* (twelfth-century source for King Arthur legends, written in Latin) | 215 |
| Jacobus de Voragine's *Golden Legend* (a collection of saints' legends, compiled in Latin in the mid-1200s) | 1,000 |
| Marco Polo's *Travels* (1299) | 150 |
| Dante's *Divine Comedy* (1321) | more than 600 |
| *The Book of Sir John Mandeville* (a travel book about a fictitious English knight, based on earlier sources and written about 1360) | more than 250 |
| Geoffrey Chaucer's *Canterbury Tales* (1386–1389) | 90 |

## IN POLO'S FOOTSTEPS

Not all useful sources of information about Polo date from the 1200s and 1300s. In more recent times, several scholar-adventurers have traveled across Asia to view for themselves the rugged mountains, vast steppes, ancient cities, and windblown deserts that Polo saw and have written books and articles about their journeys. "Much that Marco recorded hasn't changed in seven centuries," wrote the journalist Mike Edwards in 2001. In some places, Edwards observed, even the people and their customs remain the same. "In southern China I found—as he did—people with tattooed skin and teeth sheathed in gold." These eyewitness reports from later travelers, together with their drawings and photographs, help readers to imagine even more fully what Polo experienced on his historic journey.

# PRIMARY SOURCE DOCUMENT

## A PORTION OF THE EARLIEST MANUSCRIPT OF *THE TRAVELS*: LE DIVISAMENT DOU MONDE

XV. Comant les II frers et Marc [alent] avant le grant kaan eu palais

Et que voç en diroie? quant mesere Nicolau et meser Mafeu et Marc furent venus en celle grant cité, il s'en alent au mestre palais, la ou il treivent le grant kaan a mout grant conpagnie de bairon. Il s'enjenoilent devant lui et se humilient tant com il plus puent. Le grant kaan les fait drecer en estant et les recevi honorablement et lor fait grant joie et grant feste; et mout les demande de lor estre et comant il l'avoient puis fait. Les deus frers li distrent ke il l'ont moult bien fait, puis que il l'ont treuvé sain et haitiés. Adonc li preçentent les brevilés e les letres que l'apostoille le envoie, des quelz il ot grant leesse. Puis li bailent le saint oleo, de cui il fist grant joie et le tient mout chier. Le grant kaan, quant il voit Marc qui estoit jeune bachaler, il demande ki est. "Sire, fait meser Nicolao, il est mon filz et vestre home." "Bien soit il venu," fait el le gran can. Et por coi voç firoie lonc cont? sachiés tout voiremant que mout fu grant la joie et la feste ke fait le grant Kaan et toute sa cort de la venue de ceste mesajes. Et molt estoient servi et honorés de tuit. Il demorent en la cort et avoient honor sor les autre baronç."

# A LITERAL TRANSLATION

## THE DESCRIPTION OF THE WORLD

XV. How the two brothers and Marco went before the great khan at the palace

And what more shall I tell you? When Messer Nicolo and Messer Maffeo and Marco had arrived in that great city, they went to the chief palace, where they found the great khan and a very great company of barons. They knelt before him and humbled themselves as much as they could. The great khan had them stand up and received them honorably and made them great joy and great festivity. He asked much about their condition and how they had fared. The two brothers told him that they had fared very well, since they found him well and healthy. Then they presented the writings and letters which the apostle had sent, from which he had great happiness. Then they delivered to him the holy oil, of which he had great joy and held very dear. The great khan, when he saw Marco, who was a young bachelor [a young man], asked who he was. 'Sire,' said Messer Nicolo, "he is my son and your man.' 'He is very welcome,' said the great khan. And why should I make you a long story? Know in all truth that the joy and festivity were very great which the great khan and all his court made on the arrival of these envoys. And they were well served and honored by all. They stayed at court and had honor above the other barons.

131

This passage is based on the earliest surviving manuscript from the 1330s, called the F text, of *The Travels*. Scholars generally consider it the closest to the original work. Some later manuscripts contain information not in this text. Modern translations, such as Ronald Latham's, often add that information to the F text. One theory is that Polo made the additions himself after returning to Venice.

The language of the F text is medieval French as spoken in Italy. As in other medieval texts, spelling is inconsistent. Khan, for instance, is spelled both "kaan" and "can." The word for "great" (used frequently—great khan, great city, great company of barons, great joy, great festivity) is spelled both "grant" and "gran." Spelling became more fixed after the printing press arrived in Europe in the next century.

Similarly medieval is the use of Roman numerals. XV is the chapter number. Instead of "2 brothers" or "two brothers," the scribe wrote "II frers." The fact that *frer* meant both "brother" and "friar" created some confusion. A French illustrator of Polo's book assumed that Marco was accompanied by two friars. He put the Polo brothers in long robes.

The two questions in the passage are typical of the style of *The Travels*. The first, "What more shall I tell you?" suggests the storyteller is looking for the best words to describe a special scene. The other, "Why make a long story?" helps finish off the scene. Both of these expressions were used frequently in medieval popular literature, which was usually read aloud. Also typical of this medieval style are the pairs of synonyms, such as "well and healthy," "writings and letters," and "well served and honored."

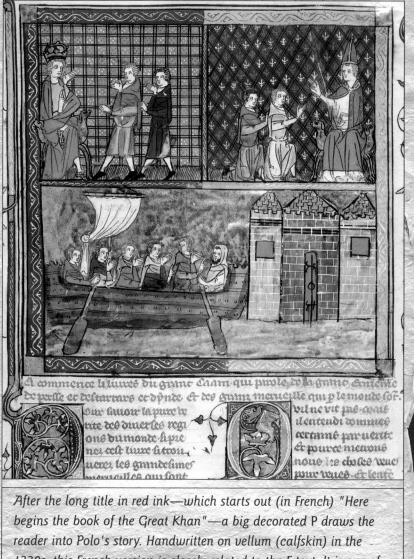

A commence li liures du grant Chaam qui parole de la grande sentence
De perse et de tartars et dynde. Et des grans meruelle qui p le monde sot.

our sauoir la pure le      vil ne vit pas crait
rite des diuerses regi       il entendi comme
ons du monde sapre          certams par uerite
nez. cest liure si trou       et pource nreons
ucres. les grandesmes       nous lre choses vues
merueilles qui sont          pur vues. et lenfie

After the long title in red ink—which starts out (in French) "Here
begins the book of the Great Khan"—a big decorated P draws the
reader into Polo's story. Handwritten on vellum (calfskin) in the
1330s, this French version is closely related to the F text. It is one of
the oldest surviving manuscripts of Polo's book and the oldest with
illustrations. Seven other works about Asia also appear in this
manuscript, which may have been prepared for King Philip VI of
France. The pictures show Nicolo and Maffeo Polo saying good-bye
to the Byzantine emperor and receiving a blessing before they sail
away from Constantinople on their first voyage east.

# TIMELINE

**1204** Venetian and French troops seize and sack Constantinople, giving Venice virtual monopoly of Black Sea trade until 1261.

*Venetian and French troops seize Constantinople in this fourteenth-century Venetian illustration.*

**1206** Genghis Khan becomes ruler of the Mongols.

**1216** Kublai Khan is born.

**1237–1242** Mongols attack Russia and eastern Europe.

**1245–1247** Friar John of Plano Carpini journeys to Karakorum in Mongolia.

**1253–1255** Friar William of Rubruck journeys to Karakorum in Mongolia.

**1254** Marco Polo is born.

| 1260 | Kublai declares himself great khan. Nicolo and Maffeo Polo begin their journey east. |
| --- | --- |
| 1261 | War breaks out between Berke Khan and Hulagu. Greek forces retake Constantinople. |
| 1264 | Kublai Khan establishes the Yuan dynasty in northern China. |
| CA. 1265 | Nicolo and Maffeo Polo visit Kublai Khan. |
| 1268 | Lorenzo Tiepolo is elected doge of Venice. Pope Clement IV dies. Commercial ties between Constantinople and Venice are resumed. |
| 1269 | Nicolo and Maffeo reach Acre and return to Venice. |
| 1271 | Nicolo, Maffeo, and Marco Polo depart on their journey to China. Pope Gregory X is elected. |

*The Polos leave for their journey to China in this fourteenth-century miniature from Jean de Mandeville's* Book of Marvels.

| | |
|---|---|
| 1273 | Kublai Khan conquers the last major Song stronghold in southern China, uniting all of China for the first time in three centuries. |
| 1275 | The Polos reach Kublai Khan's summer palace at Shangdu. |

*Kublai Khan welcomes Marco and the elder Polos in this French illustration from the fourteenth century.*

| | |
|---|---|
| 1279 | The empress dowager of China surrenders to Kublai Khan's forces, marking the end of the Song dynasty in southern China. |
| 1284 | Genoa destroys Pisan sea power. Rustichello is possibly captured in this battle. |
| 1291 | The last Crusader kingdom on the mainland of Asia is lost with the fall of Acre. |

| 1292 | The Polos leave China by sea with Princess Kokachin. |
| 1294 | Kublai Khan dies. |
| 1295 | The Polos return to Venice. |

*View of Venice in an Italian woodcut from 1486*

| 1298 | Genoa defeats Venice in a naval battle near Korcula. Marco Polo is perhaps made prisoner at this time. |
| 1299 | Venice and Genoa agree to a peace treaty and release all prisoners. |
| 1307 | Marco Polo presents a copy of *The Travels* in northern French translation to a French lord visiting Venice. He is to take the book to Charles of Valois in France. |
| 1310 | Friar Francesco Pipino begins translating *The Travels* into Latin. |
| 1324 | Marco Polo writes his will and dies on January 8. |

| 1348 | The Black Death reaches Venice and Genoa and spreads across Europe. |
|---|---|
| 1368 | The Chinese overthrow the last Mongol emperor and establish the Ming dynasty. |
| 1477 | The first printed copy of *The Travels* appears in Germany. |
| 1492 | Columbus sets sail for Cipangu and Cathay but reaches the Americas instead. |

*Columbus's three ships sail west in this twentieth-century woodcut.*

| 1559 | Giovanni Battista Ramusio's edition of *The Travels*, translated into Italian, is published in Venice. |
|---|---|

# GLOSSARY

**BLACK DEATH:** the epidemic of bubonic plague that devastated Asia and Europe in the mid-fourteenth century. The name, which comes from the black patches that form on the skin of its victims, is also used for other, later severe epidemics of plague.

**BUDDHIST:** a follower of Buddhism, a religion that grew out of the teachings of Gautama Siddhartha, known as the Buddha (ca. 560–483 B.C.), and spread through India and central and eastern Asia after his death. Buddhists seek enlightenment through mental and moral purification.

**CATAPULT:** a military device used in ancient times and during the Middle Ages to hurl missiles such as stones or spears at or over defensive walls. Catapults use the energy of tightly twisted ropes, which are suddenly released to discharge the missile with great force and speed.

**DALMATIA:** a region of southern Europe on the coast of the Adriatic Sea that extends across the modern nations of Slovenia, Croatia, Bosnia and Herzegovina, and Serbia and Montenegro. Venice began conquering Dalmatian cities in 1000 and ruled the coastal areas with its many islands and good harbors from 1420 to 1699. According to Ramusio, Marco Polo's ancestors moved from Dalmatia to Venice in 1033.

**DOGE:** the elected leader of the Venetian government. *Doge* (pronounced DOHJ) is a northern Italian dialect word for "duke." Once elected, a doge held office for life. Doges ruled Venice from 697 until 1797.

**FRIAR:** a member of a Christian religious order dedicated especially to missionary work and charity. Saint Francis of Assisi founded the first order of friars in 1209. Saint Dominic, a Spanish priest, organized a similar order in 1215. During the thirteenth century, Franciscan and Dominican friars played an important role in uniting the Roman Catholic Church within Europe and bringing Roman Catholicism to Asia.

**HYPERPYRA:** (plural of *hyperpyron*) gold coins of the Byzantine Empire that were widely used in Europe before gold coins were minted in Europe in the thirteenth century, beginning with Genoa and Florence in 1252 and Venice in 1285

**KHANATE:** a region ruled by a khan. The Mongol Empire was divided into three principal khanates and one ilkhanate (subordinate khanate).

**LIEGE MAN:** in medieval times, a nobleman who promised loyalty and service to a nobleman of higher rank or a king

**MONSOON:** seasonal winds that bring heavy rains. The Indian Ocean region has two monsoon seasons, the southwest monsoon beginning in late May or early June, and the northeast, or retreating, monsoon in October and November.

**MUSLIM:** a follower of the religious faith of Islam. Muslims believe in Allah as the sole deity and in Muhammad (ca. 570–632) as his prophet.

**PALAZZO:** (plural *palazzi*) a large, imposing building in Italy, often the residence of a wealthy nobleman and his extended family

**PAPAL LEGATE:** an official sent by the pope to a royal court or to some part of the Church to carry out a particular task. He has the authority to represent the pope or act as his agent on specific Church business.

**RIALTO**: a shortened form of the Italian words *rivo alto*, or "high bank." This high-lying area at the center of Venice is the safest from floods.

**SHAMAN:** a priest who cures the sick, solves mysteries, and controls events by his or her influence over an unseen world of gods, demons, and spirits

# WHO'S WHO?

**ARGHUN (D. 1291)** Kublai Khan's great nephew Arghun was
ilkhan of Persia after 1284. Arghun favored Christianity and
tried to gain European support for his struggle against
armies from Muslim Egypt and Syria. His son Ghazan later
converted to Islam and in 1295 made Islam the state
religion of the ilkhanate.

**BERKE KHAN (D. 1266)** A grandson of Genghis Khan, Berke
became khan of the Golden Horde, the northwestern area
of the Mongol Empire, in 1257. Nicolo and Maffeo Polo
met him in Sarai (in modern day Russia) around 1261.
Although Berke followed the Mongol policy of religious
toleration within his khanate, he sympathized with Islam.
He sided with Kublai Khan's youngest brother Arigh Boke
in the conflict for the office of great khan in 1260–1264
and fought territorial wars against cousins who were also
khans.

**MARTINO DA CANALE (CA. MID-1200S–1275)**
The Venetian historian Martino da Canale is known only
through the chronicle that he wrote, *Les Estoires de Venise
(The History of Venice)*. The chronicle, written in French,
relates the history of Venice from its origins to 1275,
focusing most of its attention on events of the thirteenth
century. Canale began writing his book, he says, in 1267.
The history breaks off in 1275, perhaps the year Canale
died.

**HULAGU (D. 1265)** Kublai Khan's younger brother Hulagu carved out a territory for himself in Persia and Mesopotamia by capturing the Islamic capital Baghdad in 1258. He challenged the Muslims in Syria as well but did not succeed in adding Syria to his ilkhanate. Polo writes of these conquests and the war against Hulagu's cousin Berke in *The Travels*.

**JOHN OF PLANO CARPINI (D. 1252)** After playing a large role in establishing the Franciscan order throughout western Europe, Friar John was sent by Pope Innocent IV to the Mongol court at Karakorum in 1245. He returned two years later and wrote *History of the Mongols*, which became the most widely known of the early accounts of the Mongols.

**KOKACHIN (CA. 1274–1296)** Kokachin was the Mongol princess whom the Polos escorted to Persia in the early 1290s. The Persian historian Rashid al-Din, author of *The History of the Mongols* in the early fourteenth century, corroborates Polo's account that the young woman was related to Arghun's wife Queen Bulagan and that she came to Persia from the court of the great khan. She married Arghun's son Ghazan in late 1293 or early 1294. According to Rashid al-Din, she died in June 1296.

**KUBLAI KHAN** (1216–1294) After his grandfather Genghis

Khan, Kublai was the greatest of the Mongol khans. An audacious commander, his military expertise was matched by his astuteness at governing the Mongol Empire, which he expanded to its largest size. Leaving the central and western khanates to their own devices, Kublai focused on developing China, which he united for the first time in almost four centuries. The empire he created survived seventy-four years after his death.

**FRANCESCO PIPINO** (LATE 1200S–EARLY 1300S) A Dominican friar in Bologna in north central Italy, Francesco Pipino was a historian who compiled a lengthy chronicle of events of the fifth to the early fourteenth centuries. During the 1310s, he wrote a shortened version of Polo's *Travels* in Latin. Almost half of the surviving manuscripts and many early printed editions of the *Travels* are based on Pipino's version.

**PRESTER JOHN,** or John the Priest, was the fictitious ruler of

a large kingdom east of the Tigris River, probably invented by a European writer living in one of the Crusader kingdoms in the mid-twelfth century. In a letter addressed to the Byzantine emperor, Prester John boasted about his great wealth and vowed to free the Holy Land from the enemies of Christianity. The letter circulated widely in Europe. Marco Polo and other Europeans traveling in Asia tried to find evidence of his mythical realm.

**GIOVANNI BATTISTA RAMUSIO** (1485–1557) A citizen of Venice, Giovanni Battista Ramusio was a diplomat and scholar with a keen interest in geography. He collected source materials of the explorations of his time, including the earliest European accounts of America, and translated them into Italian. His three-volume collection of travel narratives, *Navigazioni e Viaggi (Navigation and Travels)*, appeared in the 1550s. It includes an Italian edition of Polo's *Travels* based on Pipino's Latin translation and a lost manuscript. In a preface, Ramusio retold stories he had heard in Venice about Marco Polo.

**RUSTICHELLO OF PISA** (MID-1200S–EARLY 1300S?)

According to *The Travels*, Polo's collaborator Rustichello of Pisa was in prison with Marco Polo. Historians assume that he was captured in a battle in 1284 when Genoa defeated Pisa. Rustichello is often identified with Rusticiano of Pisa, who wrote a long story in prose about knights in King Arthur's court. Both the *Travels* and the Arthurian stories are written in a similar style. (Many other stories and histories in medieval French, however, share the same stylistic traits.)

## TEOBALDO VISCONTI (GREGORY X) (1210–1276)

Teobaldo Visconti, born in Piacenza in northern Italy, had a long career in the Roman Catholic Church. In 1271 he accompanied Prince Edward of England on a Crusade. He received word in Acre that the cardinals (who had spent three years in a deadlock) had elected him pope. As Pope Gregory X, he promoted unity with the Greek Church, resolved political conflicts within Europe, raised money for a Crusade (which never took place), reformed the papal election process, and defended Jews against unfair accusations by Christians. In 1713 he was beatified by Pope Clement XI, authorizing the title "Blessed."

**LORENZO TIEPOLO (D. 1275)** Lorenzo Tiepolo was the son of Jacopo Tiepolo, doge of Venice from 1229 to 1249. A hero in the war against Genoa, Lorenzo Tiepolo was a popular candidate for doge in 1268. Venetian nobles, fearing a dynasty would gain control of the office of doge, devised a complicated set of rules for the election. The populace was delighted when Lorenzo won anyway. The teenage Marco Polo no doubt witnessed his installation in office.

**WILLIAM OF RUBRUCK (MID-1200S)** Apparently a native of
Flanders (a medieval county including parts of Belgium,
northern France, and the Netherlands), William was a
Franciscan friar. King Louis IX of France sent him on a
mission to convert Mongols to Christianity in 1253.
William traveled to Karakorum and spent two years there.
On his return, he wrote a vivid account of his journey.

**HENRY YULE (1820–1889)** Henry Yule first read Marco Polo's

*Travels* as a young boy growing up in
Scotland. After serving as a royal engineer
in India, then a British colony, where he
oversaw construction of roads, canals,
bridges, forts, and railways, he took up
translating accounts by medieval travelers
in Asia and published a collection of them
in *Cathay and the Way Thither* in 1866. In
1867 he began his translation of Marco Polo's *Travels*,
consulting many libraries and writing to scholars all over
Europe and Asia to complete the detailed notes that make
his edition so valuable to anyone interested in Polo. Two
editions appeared in 1870 and 1874. After Yule's death, his
friend Henri Cordier supervised the publication of the third
edition in 1903.

# SOURCE NOTES

4   Martino da Canale, *Les Estoires de Venise*, ed. Alberto Limentani (Florence: Leo S. Olschki, 1972), 4, 6 (author's translation).

7   S. J. B. Barnish, trans. *The Variae of Magnus Aurelius Cassiodorus* (Liverpool: Liverpool University Press, 1992), 178.

11  Henry Treece, *The Crusades* (New York: Random House, 1962), 167.

13  Benjamin Z. Kedar, *Merchants in Crisis: Genoese and Venetian Men of Affairs and the Fourteenth-Century Depression* (New Haven, CT: Yale University Press, 1976), 58.

19  John E. Dotson, trans. and ed., *Merchant Culture in Fourteenth-Century Venice* (Binghamton, NY: Medieval and Renaissance Texts and Studies, 1994), 128.

20  Canale, 280.

22  Marco Polo, *The Travels of Marco Polo*, trans. Ronald Latham (London: Penguin Books, 1958), 213.

23  Ibid., 213.

23–24  Ibid., 221–222.

24  Ibid., 216.

24  Ibid., 214.

25  Ibid., 217.

25  Ibid., 214.

25  Ibid., 216.

25  A. C. Moule, *Quinsai: With Other Notes on Marco Polo* (Cambridge: Cambridge University Press, 1957), 23.

26  Polo, *Travels*, 219.

27  Ibid., 237.

28  Ibid.

31  Robert Silverberg, *The Realm of Prester John* (Garden City, NY: Doubleday, 1972), 42.

38  Polo, *Travels*, 154.

39  Ibid., 147.

40  Ibid., 148.

40  Ibid., 149.

41  Ibid., 119.

43  Ibid., 34.

44  Henry Yule, *The Book of Ser Marco Polo* (London: John Murray, 1903), 1:2–3.

46  Christopher Dawson, ed. *The Mongol Mission* (New York: Sheed and Ward, 1955), 90.

47  Polo, *Travels*, 34–35.

48  Ibid., 35.

48  Ibid.

50  Ibid., 37.

50  Ibid.

51  Metropolitan Museum of Art, "In the Footsteps of Marco Polo," *Metropolitan Museum of Art*, (2000), http://www.metmuseum.org/explore/Marco/index.html (December 27, 2006).

53  Polo, *Travels*, 39.

53  Ibid.

53  Ibid., 46.

54  Yule, 1:20n.

54  Polo, *Travels*, 58.

55  Ibid., 33.

55  Ibid., 65.

59  Ibid., 66.

59  Ibid., 69.

59  Ibid., 74.

60  Ibid., 77–78.

60  Ibid., 66.

60  Harry Rutstein and Joanne Kroll, *In the Footsteps of Marco Polo* (New York: Viking Press, 1980), 126.

60  Polo, *Travels*, 80.

60  Ibid.

62  Mike Edwards, The Adventures of Marco Polo," Part 2, *National Geographic*, June 2001, 25.

62–64  Polo, *Travels*, 85.

63  Ibid., 80.

65  Ibid., 85.

66  Ibid., 41–42.

66  Ibid., 108.

66–67  Marco Polo, *The Description of the World*, trans. and ed., A. C. Moule and Paul Pelliot (London: G. Routledge, 1938), 1:185.

67–68  Polo, *Travels*, 40.

68  Ibid.

68  Marco Polo, *Milione: Le Divisament dou Monde*, ed. Gabriella Ronchi (Milan: Mondadori, 1982), 317 (author's translation).

70  Polo, *Travels*, 40.

71  John D. Langlois, Jr., ed. *China under Mongol Rule* (Princeton, NJ: Princeton University Press, 1981), 4.

74  Polo, *Travels*, 40.

74–75  Ibid., 41.

75  Ibid.

76  Ibid.

78–79  Ibid., 149.

79  Ibid., 201.

80  Ibid., 99–100.

81  Ibid., 42.

81–82  Ibid., 211.

83  Ibid., 152.

83  Ibid., 156.

84  Ibid.

86  Ibid., 344–345.

86  Ibid., 42.

87  Ibid.

87–88  Ibid., 43.

88  Ibid., 244.

89  Ibid., 249.

89  Ibid., 251.

89  Ibid., 258.

89–90  Ibid., 256.

90  Ibid., 300.

91  Ibid., 253.

91  Ibid., 256.

91  Ibid., 287, 288, and 307.

92  Ibid., 259.

93  Ibid., 283.

93  Ibid., 260.

93  Ibid., 45.

95  Yule, 1:4.

95  Ibid., 5.

96  Ibid.

98  Ibid., 6

99  Polo, *Travels*, 33.

100–101  Ibid.

101  Ibid., 189.

102  Yule, 1:120.

102  Ibid., 119.

102  Yule, 2:525.

103  Yule, 1:54.

106  Fray Bartolomé de las Casas, *The Diario of Christopher Columbus's First Voyage to America 1492–1493*, ed. Oliver Dunn and James E. Kelley, Jr., (Norman: University of Oklahoma Press, 1989), 111, 113.

109  Robert S. Lopez and Irving W. Raymond, eds., *Medieval Trade in the Mediterranean World* (New York: Columbia University Press, 1955), 357.

112  John Larner, *Marco Polo and the Discovery of the World* (New Haven, CT: Yale University Press, 1999), 144.

112  Polo, *Travels*, 244.

114  Larner, 163.

115 Leonardo Olschki, *Marco Polo's Asia*, trans. John A. Scott (Berkeley: University of California Press, 1960), 136.

115 Ibid., 146.

123 Polo, *The Description*, 1:5.

129 Edwards, Pt. 1, 9.

130 Polo, *Milione*, 317.

# BIBLIOGRAPHY

## EDITIONS OF MARCO POLO'S BOOK

*The Book of Ser Marco Polo the Venetian.* Translated and edited by Henry Yule. 3rd rev. ed., 2 vols. London: John Murray, 1903.

*The Description of the World.* Translated and edited by A. C. Moule and Paul Pelliot. 3 vols. London: G. Routledge, 1938.

*Milione, Le Divisament dou Monde.* Edited by Gabriella Ronchi. Milan: Arnoldo Mondadori, 1982.

*The Travels of Marco Polo.* Translated by Ronald Latham. London: Penguin Books, 1958.

## PRIMARY SOURCES

Canale, Martino da. *Les Estoires de Venise.* Edited by Alberto Limentani. Florence: Leo S. Olschki, 1972.

Dawson, Christopher, ed. *The Mongol Mission.* New York: Sheed and Ward, 1955.

Dotson, John E., trans. and ed. *Merchant Culture in Fourteenth-Century Venice.* Binghamton, NY: Medieval and Renaissance Texts and Studies, 1994.

Lopez, Robert S., and Irving W. Raymond, eds. *Medieval Trade in the Mediterranean World.* New York: Columbia University Press, 1955.

Orlandini, G., ed. "Marco Polo e la sua famiglia." *Archivio Veneto Tridentino IX* (1926), 1–68.

Silverberg, Robert. *The Realm of Prester John.* Garden City, NY: Doubleday, 1972.

## SECONDARY SOURCES

Abu-Lughod, Janet L. *Before European Hegemony: The World System 1250–1350.* New York: Oxford University Press, 1989.

Ashtor, Eliyahu. *Levant Trade in the Later Middle Ages.* Princeton, NJ: Princeton University Press, 1983.

Bohong, Jin. *In the Footsteps of Marco Polo.* Beijing: New World Press, 1989.

Boulnois, Luce. *Silk Road: Monks, Warriors and Merchants on the Silk Road.* Translated by Helen Loveday. Hong Kong: Odyssey Books, 2004.

Critchley, John. *Marco Polo's Book.* Aldershot, UK: Variorum, 1992.

Edwards, Mike. "The Adventures of Marco Polo." Pts. 1–3. *National Geographic,* May–July 2001, 2–31, 20–45, and 26–47.

———. "The Great Khans." *National Geographic,* February 1997, 2–35.

Franke, Herbert. *China under Mongol Rule.* Brookfield, VT: Variorum, 1994.

Gernet, Jacques. *Daily Life in China on the Eve of the Mongolian Invasion, 1250–1276.* Translated by H. M. Wright. New York: Macmillan, 1962.

Grousset, René. *The Empire of the Steppes: A History of Central Asia.* Translated by Naomi Walford. New Brunswick, NJ: Rutgers University Press, 1970.

Kedar, Benjamin Z. *Merchants in Crisis: Genoese and Venetian Men of Affairs and the Fourteenth-Century Depression.* New Haven, CT: Yale University Press, 1976.

Lach, Donald F. *Asia in the Making of Europe.* Vol. 1, pt. 1. *The Century of Discovery.* Chicago: University of Chicago Press, 1965.

Lane, Frederic. *Venice, a Maritime Republic.* Baltimore: Johns Hopkins University Press, 1973.

Langlois, John D., Jr., ed. *China under Mongol Rule.* Princeton, NJ: Princeton University Press, 1981.

Larner, John. *Marco Polo and the Discovery of the World.* New Haven, CT: Yale University Press, 1999.

Moule, A. C. *Quinsai: With Other Notes on Marco Polo.* Cambridge: Cambridge University Press, 1957.

Norwich, John Julius. *Venice: The Rise to Empire.* London: Allen Lane, 1977.

Olschki, Leonardo. *Marco Polo's Asia.* Translated by John A. Scott. Berkeley: University of California Press, 1960.

Pelliot, Paul. *Notes on Marco Polo.* 2 vols. Paris: Impr. nationale, 1959–1973.

Rossabi, Morris. *Khubilai Khan, His Life and Times*. Berkeley: University of California Press, 1988.

Runciman, Steven. *A History of the Crusades*. Vol. 3. *The Kingdom of Acre and the Later Crusades*. Cambridge: Cambridge University Press, 1954.

Rutstein, Harry, and Joanne Kroll. *In the Footsteps of Marco Polo*. New York: Viking Press, 1980.

Scammell, G. V. *The World Encompassed: The First European Maritime Empires*. Berkeley: University of California Press, 1981.

Slessarev, Vsevolod. *Prester John: The Letter and the Legend*. Minneapolis: University of Minnesota Press, 1959.

Zorzi, Alvise, ed. *Marco Polo: Venezia e l'Oriente*. Milan: Electa, 1981.

# FURTHER READING

Dramer, Kim. *Kublai Khan*. New York: Chelsea House, 1990.

Hull, Mary. *The Mongol Empire*. San Diego: Lucent Books, 1998.

Pelta, Kathy. *Discovering Christopher Columbus*. Minneapolis: Twenty-First Century Books, 1991.

Siebold, Thomas. *The 1200s*. San Diego: Greenhaven Press, 2001.

Stefoff, Rebecca. *Marco Polo and the Medieval Explorers*. New York: Chelsea House, 1992.

Twist, Clint. *Marco Polo, Overland to Medieval China*. Austin, TX: Raintree Steck-Vaughn, 1994.

Worth, Richard. *The Great Empire of China and Marco Polo in World History*. Berkeley Heights, NJ: Enslow, 2003.

## FICTION SET IN THIRTEENTH-CENTURY CHINA

McCaughrean, Geraldine. *The Kite Rider*. New York: HarperCollins, 2002.

Wilson, Diane. *I Rode a Horse of Milk White Jade*. New York: HarperCollins, 2000.

# WEBSITES

Hubbard, John. "Marco Polo's Asia."
http://www.tk421.net/essays/polo.html This is an overview of Marco
Polo's travels and legacy.

"In the Footsteps of Marco Polo." *Metropolitan Museum of Art.*
http://www.metmuseum.org/explore/Marco/index.html Maps,
artwork, and artifacts trace Polo's journey across Asia.

Keller, Carol A. and San Antonio College History Department. "The
Mongol Empire."
http:www.accd.edu/sac/history/Keller/Mongols/empire.html This is
the place to find reprints of primary sources of various aspects of
Mongol history.

Knox, E. L. Skip. "The Middle Ages, Trails, Venice." *Boise State
University.* http://history.boisestate.edu/westciv/medieval/trails/Venice
The site contains pictures of and questions about San Marco and the
bronze horses.

"Kublai Khan in Battle, 1287." *Eyewitness to History.*
www.eyewitnesstohistory.com/khan.htm A passage from *The Travels* is
included in this website.

"Marco Polo and His Travels." *Silk Road Foundation.* http://www.silk-
road.com/artl/marcopolo.shtml This website contains an article on
Marco Polo with links to additional articles on "Pax Mongolica,"
paper money, friars John of Plano Carpini and William Rubruck, and
other topics related to east-west trade on the Silk Road from 959
B.C.E. to modern times.

"Marco Polo Homepage." *Susquehanna University.*
http:www.susqu.edu/history/medtrav/marcopolo/default.htm This
website includes a brief profile, map, and bibliography.

"The Mongols in World History." *Asia for Educators, Columbia University.*
http://afe.easia.columbia.edu/mongols/ This site explores the
significance of Mongols and includes maps, images, and information
on Marco Polo and Kublai Khan.

# INDEX

# ABOUT THE AUTHOR

Diana Childress has published four nonfiction books for young people and writes about history, archaeology, art, and literature for children's magazines and textbooks. A native of Texas, she grew up in Mexico and returned to the United States for college. Since earning her Ph.D. in medieval English literature, she has taught college English and worked as a school librarian in New York City.

# PHOTO ACKNOWLEDGMENTS

The images in this book are used with the permission of: © Réunion des Musées Nationaux/Art Resource, NY, p. 5; © Laura Westlund/Independent Picture Service, pp. 6, 42–43, 56–57; © Roger-Viollet, p. 8; © North Wind Picture Archives, pp. 11, 78, 98, 138, 144 (top); © Erich Lessing/Art Resource, NY, pp. 13, 45, 137; © Mimmo Jodice/CORBIS, p. 14; © Cameraphoto/Art Resource, NY, p. 17; © The Art Archive/Querini Stampalia Foundation Venice/Dagli Orti, p. 18; © Werner Forman/Art Resource, NY, pp. 24, 82; © The Art Archive/Freer Gallery of Art, p. 27; © Art Archive/Bodleian Library Oxford, pp. 30, 134; © SuperStock, Inc./SuperStock, pp. 32, 33, 49, 67, 69, 128, 136; © Getty Images, pp. 36, 52, 58, 100, 144 (bottom), 145, 146; © Giraudon/Art Resource, NY, pp. 38, 96; Private Collection/Bridgeman Art Library, pp. 40, 105; © Keren Su/CORBIS, pp. 61, 62; © Snark/Art Resource, NY, p. 63; © The Art Archive/British Museum, p. 64; © Bettmann/CORBIS, p. 68; © Christel Gerstenberg/CORBIS, p. 73; © Archivo Iconografico, SA/CORBIS, p. 75; © The Granger Collection, New York, pp. 81, 84, 92, 107, 135, 143; Bibliotheque Nationale, Paris/Archives Charmet/Bridgeman Art Library, p. 87; © Art Media/Heritage-Images/The Image Works, p. 90; © Bridgeman Art Library, London/SuperStock, p. 94; © The Art Archive/Biblioteca Nazionale Marciana Venice/Dagli Orti, p. 110; © HIP/Art Resource, NY, p. 121; © The British Library/HIP/The Image Works, p. 133; National Portrait Gallery, London, p. 147.

Cover: © North Wind Picture Archives.